BRITISH MOTOR SCOOTERS 1946–1970

The
complete history
of British Motor
Scooters made from
1946 to 1970...

BRITISH MOTOR
SCOOTERS 1940s

DEA
850

AUTOMOBILE PALACE · LIMITED
Managing Director: TOM NORTON
LLANDRINDOD WELLS
TELEPHONE—2215 (3 lines)

Published in the United Kingdom in 2012 by **Bavarov Ltd**.

WWW.BRITISHSCOOTERS.COM

British Library Cataloguing-in-Publication Data

A catalogue record for this book is available from the British Library.

ISBN 978-0-9573144-0-5

British Leadership - Superb Quality

PRETTY
AS A
PICTURE

From the sleek lines of the main body and side panels to the built-in " dual " rear lamp units, the
" Flamenco " is not only pretty, but efficient as well.

Easily seen from this illustration are the large glove-compartment and lockable tool-box which
are situated directly below the dashboard, incorporating an ammeter; the large expanse of foot
platform gives ample foot room.

BRITISH MOTOR SCOOTERS 1950s

FOREWORD

The British motorcycle industry, by and large, missed the scooter 'boom' by dragging its heels in a pointer of what was to come in the world of bigger wheeled motorised two-wheeler, just a few years later. Though that sounds a somewhat negative tone on which to introduce a book about those scootering efforts, the fact that the period wasn't an unmitigated success doesn't make it any less worthy of research and documentation.

Though there were many noteworthy and fascinating British attempts, as detailed in this diligently and carefully collated volume, the British scooter movement has no name as synonymous and intrinsically linked with life on smaller wheels as say Vespa or Lambretta.

But it's fascinating to examine the efforts which were produced, whether they were a success or not. So many were actually really worthy of praise, with innovative thinking and 'starting with a blank sheet of paper' designs abounding, with designers and engineers given (and exploiting) a freedom that didn't exist in other areas of two-wheeled industry.

There are, though, abounding stories of missed opportunities – for example, BSA had its Dinghy on test during the Second World War and could have been there at the cessation of hostilities, while its Beeza could have appeared just a few years later. Both a case of could have been, should have been.

Likewise, the technically excellent but ill-timed and 'over engineered' Velocette Viceroy, a quite superb piece of kit but which arrived onto a market which neither requested or wanted it.

From 1946 to 1970 is the period covered here, which fairly neatly falls either side of the year when most two wheelers were registered in the UK, 1959. Of course, 1959 was also the year when the Alec Issigonis designed Mini was launched onto an eager market, a move which arguably had a greater impact on the scooter buyer than the motorcycle purchaser; here was a clean, attractively styled, modern, well thought out 'small package' which made the most of the available space and ran on little wheels – surely, that's what scooters were too?

Robin Spalding is just the man to document this fantastic period. Endlessly enthusiastic about scooters in general and British built examples in particular, Robin has become a fixture at shows up and down the country, with, in recent years, his fascinating (and ever-expanding) collection of Old Albion's offerings invariably earning him a 'Best scooter' award in the nation's largest classic shows. A man who has put forward the best the British industry could muster, presented in an attractive way, for the interest and entertainment of others – similar to what he is doing with this book.

James Robinson
Editor, The Classic MotorCycle

BRITISH MOTOR SCOOTERS 1960s

CONTENTS

Continues overleaf...

Phoenix scooter • Page 61

PROTOTYPES [not in collection]

BSA Beeza • Page 157

Scooter News magazine – see page 45

INTRODUCTION

There are a number of books available on motor scooters that attempt to cover world scooter production from the early 1900s to date, this is obviously a very challenging task with extremely wide boundaries. This book covers in detail the British scooters made from post World War Two to the time of the last scooter made in Britain in 1970. In addition to the scooters that went into production I have attempted to capture all the makers who made a prototype machine or a small batch of scooters. Also included are a few machines that were made in other countries, and others that do not possess all the features of the true definition of a scooter but are in some way still part of the British scooter scene. For the period under review – 1946 to 1970 – I have attempted to cover every scooter/scooterette listed in the scooter magazine price lists including the quirky and those that perhaps did not really deserve a mention. However, I feel they too should take their place in history. Instead of the A-Z format I have prepared the book in chronological order based on production years, this allows additional information concerning other similar forms of two-wheeled transport and comments on the situation in other countries to be included at the appropriate time.

My own collection of British scooters includes over 40 models from 25 different manufacturers. My interest in mopeds and scooters began in 1957 before my sixteenth birthday – I worked in a paper shop and was able to look through all the important magazines on the subject. Much of my research has come from these magazines of the 1950/60s that I have been able to purchase over recent years – the most significant magazines are Power and Pedal, Scooter and Three Wheeler and Scooter World. In addition both the major motorcycle magazines quickly included a scooter section when they became so popular in the late 1950s.

At the age of sixteen I owned an Italian Guizzo three-speed moped in red and cream, a year or so later I bought a second hand British Dayton Albatross 250cc scooter and two years later I exchanged it for a pre-war car. It was not until 1999 I purchased another scooter that started a collection of European scooters and mopeds, in 2007 the collecting theme changed to concentrate on just British scooters.

My first two-wheeler, a 1959 Italian Guizzo Turismo moped in flashy red and cream.

Many people think that the first motor scooter was the Italian Piaggio Vespa of 1946 – this was in fact the start of the third scooter boom – I have therefore started with information on the scooters made following World War One, those made in America after the Great Depression, and the Military scooters used in the Second World War. There is an excellent book about 'Whatever happened to the British Motorcycle Industry' by Bert Hopwood – I hope this book goes some way in explaining whatever happened to the British Motor Scooter Industry.

I

As the subject of British scooters is somewhat serious I have introduced a little humour to the book with a number of cartoon type pictures. The 1950/60s scooter magazines had many cartoons on their pages with the Scooter World magazine even placing a cartoon now and again on the front cover. Something that could easily have been the subject of a cartoon was the British scooter I desperately wanted at the age of 14½. It was the 'Streets ahead' Scoo-Ped made by Elswick-Hopper at a cost of 33 Guineas.

A very serious author with his sister Jennifer on a 1959 Dayton Albatross in 1961.

THE AUTOMOBILE ASSOCIATION
RECEIVED
24 JUN 1960
TECHNICAL LIBRARY

turismo

£75 - 12

ENGINE
The reliable « Morini Franco » 2 stroke, 3 speed 35-40 m.p.h. - Petrol cons. 200 m.p.g.

FRAME
Pressed steel - telescopic front forks - swinging arm - rear suspension.

WHEELS
Chrome - with powerful central brakes.

Guizzo 48 CC.

Brochure for my 1959 Guizzo moped .

Streets ahead, — in styling !
Teenagers will go for its aerodynamic design and streamlined good looks, the lustrous pearl-grey colour scheme with rich gold hand-lining!

Streets ahead, — in comfort !
Older people will like the low build for easy mounting, the special Sturmey-Archer 3-speed gear to take all the push out of pedalling!

Streets ahead, — in construction !
Mechanical minds will note the robust tubular frame and tough Fibreglass bodywork — practically indestructible, proof against denting, and bumps. SCOO-PED is 100% rust proof and easy to clean with a damp sponge.

Streets ahead, — in safety !
All will approve the excellent braking system, the extra-wide skid-free tyres which prevent wobbling, give greater stability. The latest Lucas battery lighting set is built-in to provide the best in installed lighting.

Streets ahead, — in convenience !
Women will appreciate the wrap-around skirt guard, the wind-and-weather protection of the front panelling, and provision for special shopping basket. SCOO-PED can be parked in the open by day and night without harm.

Streets ahead, — in economy !
All the elegance and comfort of a scooter, combined with the ease and economy of cycling!

The Elswick-Hopper Scoo-Ped, a teenager's dream however not a success due to its heavy weight and the difficulties of getting at the moving parts.

Albatross "*Continental*"

£235 - 0 - 0 TWIN

Basic £188 - 7 - 7   P/Tax £46 - 12 - 5

POST WORLD WAR ONE SCOOTERS

The motor scooter boom following World War Two was the third – the second was in America in the 1930s following the Great Depression and the first followed the Great War of 1914/18. During this war many people had experienced their first use of motorised vehicles and were keen to have their own means of personal transport back in civvy street. This included the ladies who by this time were attending major motorcycle racing programmes and looking for a means of transport for shopping trips and visiting friends.

The name 'motor scooter' is amply illustrated by one of the first designs – the Autoped – it looked just like a child's scooter with small wheels, low platform and standing room only. A number of these early scooters were quite crude and rushed to the market to satisfy demand – they lasted just a short time and unfortunately gave the motor scooter a bad name on its first outing. However, some were different and did have limited success. The Autoped was an American design produced from 1916 and made under licence by the British company Imperial Motor Industries Ltd., it had a 155cc engine positioned on the left of the front wheel with the fuel tank above the wheel. The standing rider pushed the steering bar forward to engage the clutch to move off and backwards to disengage the clutch and apply the front (and only) brake. The machine had a top speed of 10 mph and was normally illustrated with a well dressed lady rider with her dress flowing in the breeze.

A more expensive British scooter of the period was the ABC Skootamota designed by Granville Bradshaw and on the market from 1919 to 1923. The four-stroke 125cc engine was positioned over the rear wheel with the petrol and oil tanks

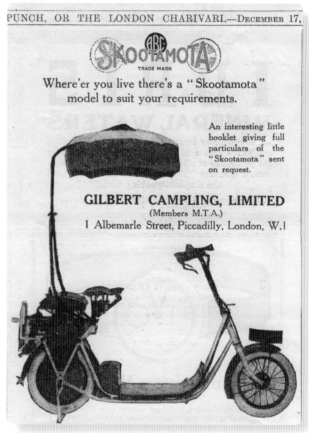

The Skootamota was the best selling machine during the period.

above. The scooter had a tubular frame with both front and rear brakes and – a saddle. The Skootamota was the best selling machine during the period, gave ample room for a ladies large dress and moved at up to 15 mph between home and the shops. It even came with a sunshade as an extra. The Skootamota competed with a number of similar scooters of the time including the Autoglide, Kenilworth Kingsbury, and one made by Alvis – manufacturers of engines and motorcars – known as the Stafford Pup. However, one it could not compete with was the Unibus.

The Unibus scooter was manufactured by the Gloucestershire Aircraft Company and could be easily mistaken for a scooter designed in the 1950s. The text from an advertisement in the magazine Punch of September 1920 states 'The UNIBUS has been called the 'Car on Two Wheels' because it is built just like a car – with front and rear springs, two-speed gearbox and clutch, shaft transmission, and even a starting handle. The UNIBUS is as handy as a bicycle and as comfortable as a car. The UNIBUS will travel over 80 miles per gallon and at 30mph'. Miss Violet Loraine looks most pleased with her scooter.

The machine was based on a pressed steel chassis with a fully enclosed body and good weather protection, these design features were firsts for the motor scooter. The engine was a 269cc two-stroke mounted behind the front wheel and started with a car type handle – a shaft drive was then used to drive a two-speed gearbox on the rear wheel. The scooter also had front and rear brakes plus front and rear suspension using quarter elliptical springs. Further innovations were included in the Unibus which of course gave it one enormous disadvantage – a Cyclecar could be bought for a similar sum of £75. It is now undoubtedly the most sought after scooter from the first scooter boom period of 1916 to the mid 1920s.

The UNIBUS is as handy as a bicycle and as comfortable as a car.

Miss Violet Loraine on a "Unibus." Notice how complete the protection for both rider and mechanism.

The UNIBUS is specially suitable for ladies. It is ideal for visiting, for pic-nics, for tennis parties, while the roomy compartment underneath the seat is available for carrying parcels on shopping expeditions, safely, cleanly, and out of sight.

The UNIBUS is manufactured by The Gloucestershire Aircraft Company, Limited, Sunningend Works, Cheltenham.

AMERICAN SCOOTERS FROM THE MID 1930s

In 1935 with America in the grip of The Great Depression E.Foster Salsbury thought that a cheap form of personal transport was a necessity. He had seen the feminist aviator Amelia Earhart trundling along an airstrip on a twenty-five year old Motoped scooter and considered a modern version would be the way ahead. By the following year the first Salsbury scooter called the Motor Glide was on the market and the second scooter boom had began. Very soon after this the American engine manufacturer Cushman built their first Auto-Glide scooter, Salsbury then improved their design with their Self-shifting Transmission – this was the start of the automatic transmission using a belt system with two adjustable vee-pullies that is now used on all the modern twist and go scooters.

The flood gates then opened and many American companies began producing motor scooters including the Rock-Ola company famous for their jukeboxes. The first machines were practical but mainly unattractive – however, looks did improve with Salsbury's 1937 Aero Model and a very pretty and curvaceous model made in 1939 called the Crocker Scootabout.

1937 Cushman Auto-Glide.

The automatic 1937 Salsbury Aero Model.

A number of scooters, including Cushmans, were made during the war years for civilians involved with the war effort and production began again after the war and went on into the 1960s. A great number of scooters including the Cushman Eagle – styled like a mini Harley Davidson – were the cool form of transport for High School kids. In 1960 Harley Davidson did make a scooter called the Topper, although said to be 'Tops in beauty and tops in performance' it was a very square-ish design with a 165cc engine giving a top speed of just 45 mph.

The last scooter produced by the pioneering Salsbury company was sensational – it was very large, streamlined and called model 85. It had aircraft type stub axles for the wheels making wheel changes as easy as a car, it obviously had their automatic transmission with just two pedal control, stop and go. The final Salsbury 85s were made in 1949, however, Cushman scooters lasted until 1961 when the company began distributing the Italian Vespa.

The Doodle Bug sold through Gambles Stores in America in the mid 1940s.

The design of the American scooters had an influence on a number of the European and Japanese scooters made immediately following World War Two in the same way the Motoped had influenced E.Foster Salsbury in the mid 1930s. Very few American scooters were sold in Britain – a small number of Harley Davidson Toppers were sold in the early 1960s by a Harley Davidson specialist in London, the cost of this square 45 mph machine was listed as £252.17.4 when a BSA Sunbeam, all curves and 70 mph, could be yours for just £198.0.0, the Topper did of course have automatic transmission.

The wonderful 1947 Salsbury model 85 restored and owned by Philip Olivier, Belgium.

WORLD WAR TWO MILITARY SCOOTERS

Like many other types of transport the motor scooter was called into active service during World War Two, the British Military scooter was known as the Welbike. Lieutenant – Colonel John R.V.Dolphin was Director of the Research and Design Establishment of the Special Operations Executive at Welwyn, Hertfordshire, the centre was responsible for the development and production of weapons to assist their special agents during the war. Many of the items produced used the 'Wel' name from the location at Welwyn – alongside the Welbike the centre produced a Welgun, a Welmine and a Welman (a one man submarine). The Special Operations Executive saw the need for a motorised vehicle giving troops a fast departure from a landing zone, the specification required the vehicle to be lightweight, to fit into a 15" diameter 6'-0" long cylindrical canister for parachute drops and assembled in the shortest possible time for riding and rapid dispersal.

The design for the Welbike had a $\frac{5}{8}$" diameter welded duplex frame housing a 98cc Villiers Junior De-luxe engine with a clutch and single speed. It had spoked wheels having a tyre size of 12 ½" x 2 ¼" and of course folding handlebars and a seat stem that moved down into a tube to give the necessary dimensions to fit into the drop canister.

1942-43 Military Welbike with a 98cc Villiers engine, shown at a classic bike show in 2008.

The 98cc Villiers engine had been used in Autocycles before the war but the Welbike was modified slightly and given adequate clearances – there was certainly no time for running-in requirements! The fuel tank was positioned in front of the engine at the same height so no gravity feed to the carburettor was possible, therefore a pressurised system using a hand pump and a safety relief valve was used, the tank held six and a half pints giving a range of approximately 90 miles.

The machine weighed just 70lbs and it was claimed that an experienced rider could remove the bike from the canister, and with a paddle start, ride off into the sunset in just 11 seconds giving the rapid dispersal required with speeds of up to 30mph. For simplicity and weight saving measures the little scooter had no kick-start, no front brake and no front mudguard. The normal colour for the Welbike was olive drab with fuel filling instruction transfers and the War Department number stencilled on the tank.

The Department placed orders for the manufacture with the Excelsior Motor Co. Ltd of Birmingham – the first order was given in August 1942 and the last in June 1943, it is estimated that a total of 3,640 machines were made. Although claims were made that the Welbike was used in most combat areas of the world the major use by the military seems to have been on airfields and ships, and for "fast" message carrying duties.

After the war many Welbikes were sold as War Department surplus with the majority being sold to the USA as a novelty machine. Due to the design having no front brake the vehicle did not meet the Construction and Use Regulations in Britain, obviously a few did find there way on the roads and some were used by the 'White Helmets' display team as a fun element.

Cushman Airborne Scooter

MODEL 53A

NOW Available for Civilian Use

AT LAST a closely guarded war secret can be told. During the preparation of the American Forces for the invasion of Germany, we were called upon to design a special Cushman Motor Scooter for the United States Army Paratroopers and since our victory in Germany, this very important piece of war transportation is available for civilian use.

We are proud to present this Model "53A" Airborne Motor Scooter to the American public for their use in safe, economical and enjoyable transportation.

This Airborne Scooter was designed and built to withstand the rigors of war. To this sturdiness has been added all the features of our regular scooter to assure you of an easy, comfortable ride.

The picture above illustrates how the Cushman Airborne Scooters are dropped by parachute from planes in the sky to give the paratroopers extra maneuverability on the ground.

The "Airborne" scooter was designed and built sturdy enough to withstand the severe shock and jolt in landing. Powered by the famous "Husky" engine, this machine travels over all kinds of terrain, through mud, sand, up steep inclines and even through underbrush. It has met the rigorous tests of war and earned an enviable record for speedy, dependable transportation at an amazingly low cost.

IN THE CITY

ON THE FARM

CUSHMAN MOTOR WORKS
LINCOLN 1, NEBRASKA

The Welbike was the only machine designed to be dropped in the canister but other lightweights were also made for airborne use. James had a 122cc Villiers motorbike with folding bars and footrests known as the 'Clockwork Mouse' and Royal Enfield made the 'Flying Flea' again using a 125cc engine, however the largest number of two-wheelers produced for Paratroopers was the humble folding bicycle made by BSA.

Other countries also had their military scooters, the Italian forces had a small 125cc machine made by Societa Volugrafo of Turin and called the Aermoto and the Americans had the Cushman model 53 Airborne. The Cushman was a much larger machine

than the Aermoto and Welbike and was in fact a strengthened and stripped Model 34 civilian scooter – to help with the availability of spare parts it ran on the same tyres as an American spotter aircraft. As with the improved Welbike (sold as a Corgi) the Cushman also went into civilian use after the war – a change in springs and electrics and with the application of a few transfers it was ready for the post war roads.

Some countries continued to use military scooters after the war, the French made an enormous Bernardet scooter with towing hook for a large gun, and also the French ACMA Vespa was produced capable of carrying a bazooka and six shells.

SWALLOW GADABOUT 1946-51

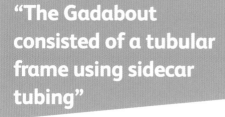

"The Gadabout consisted of a tubular frame using sidecar tubing"

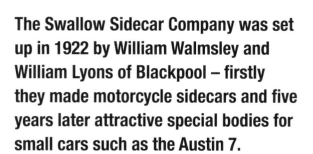

The Swallow Sidecar Company was set up in 1922 by William Walmsley and William Lyons of Blackpool – firstly they made motorcycle sidecars and five years later attractive special bodies for small cars such as the Austin 7.

By 1935 the company split with William Lyons moving solely into cars with SS Cars Ltd (later to become Jaguar Cars). After the war in 1945 the sidecar manufacture was taken over by the aircraft firm of Helliwells based on Walsall Airport in Staffordshire run by Ernest Sanders under the company name of Swallow Coachbuilding Company (1935) Ltd. During World War Two Frank Rainbow an engineer with the Bristol Aircraft Company had seen the American Cushman Model 53 Airbourne scooter in use on our airstrips, he quickly produced designs and a sales brochure for his own scooter called the Rainbow.

He had also met Ernest Sanders who was looking for work to follow on from Helliwells war effort.

Introducing . . .

The "RAINBOW"

The original scooter designed by Frank Rainbow.

Agreement was soon reached for the scooter to be produced by Sanders, however, modifications had to be made to Rainbow's initial designs to reduce manufacturing costs and the price of the scooter.

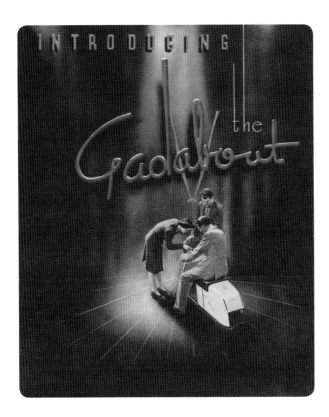

The scooter was called the Swallow Gadabout, the Gadabout consisted of a tubular ladder frame using sidecar tubing coming up in the front to support the steering head, two smaller tubes formed the front forks at the bottom end and the two handlebars at the top. A removable steel structure with simple body panels and the rider's seat was bolted to the main frame. With a top speed of 35 m.p.h. Rainbow stated no suspension was necessary as road shocks would be taken by the well upholstered large sprung seat and the 4.00 in. x 8.00 in. tyres. Although not his first choice Rainbow settled for a pre-war Villiers 9D 122cc engine which had been used during the war in the James military motorcycle, however, these units could only be supplied at the rate of 50 per month. The 9D unit had a three speed gearbox operated by an external car type gearlever on the

right hand side above the kick-start. The engine had twin exhaust ports and exhaust gases were passed through the two main frame members with a silencer under the engine.

The scooter came with 6v direct lighting, a speedo, a bulb horn and a string bag behind the legshield to bring home 'produce' from the home farm. Engine cooling was tackled with a scoop under the frame in the legshield area and various vents including some on both sides of the rear number plate to release the hot air. This was to be a problem.

The Gadabout was produced from November 1946 at the Helliwell factory in Treforest, Wales north of Cardiff, testing took place around the factory and in Stafford but failed to highlight the overheating problem when living and riding in town.

The solution could be solved immediately by the owner removing the cover over the front of the engine, however, a better solution was the installation of a cooling fan driven off the crankshaft. A MK I scooter with the cooling fan modification is known as a Gadabout MK I½. In 1948 the Company was sold to Tube Investments and by 1949 they

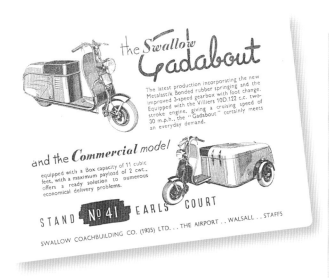

the **Swallow** **Gadabout**

The latest production incorporating the new Metalastik Bonded rubber springing and the improved 3-speed gearbox with foot change. Equipped with the Villiers 10D.122 c.c. two-stroke engine, giving a cruising speed of 30 m.p.h., the "Gadabout" certainly meets an everyday demand.

and the **Commercial** *model*

equipped with a Box capacity of 11 cubic feet, with a maximum payload of 2 cwt., offers a ready solution to numerous economical delivery problems.

STAND **Nº 41** EARLS COURT

SWALLOW COACHBUILDING CO. (1935) LTD... THE AIRPORT.. WALSALL.. STAFFS

announced the Gadabout MK II with a post war 10D Villiers 122cc engine with foot gear change, a car type cooling fan, a tilting body at the rear to assist wheel changes, rubber-in-torsion front suspension and a 6v battery for improved lighting.

Rainbow still felt the front suspension was unnecessary but a few Italian Vespa and Lambretta scooters were appearing with this de-luxe feature so Helliwells thought it the way to go. The solo machine found use with the G.P.O., Public Utilities and Police Forces and from early days the Commercial unit with a sidecar welded to the scooter frame was used by utility companies and tradesmen such as bakers and grocers.

The price of a Gadabout MK II at the time of the 1949 Earls Court Show was £103.1.10 including purchase tax, and the sidecar unit £115 (due to commercial use purchase tax was not payable on the sidecar unit). Like high class automobiles the price of the Gadabout was never quoted in their colour magazine advertisements, also like the early Fords for simplicity of production the Gadabouts all left the factory in Wales in black – however, colours were added at customers request to the easily removable back body section and legshields at the Walsall Works or the Swallow dealers. At the 1949 Show three scooters were on the Swallow stand in black with primrose yellow, pale blue and maroon as a second colour.

In 1951 the Mark III Gadabout Major sidecar outfit could be purchased with a Villiers 197cc engine for £156 – but unfortunately time was running out for the Gadabout.

However, the Swallow brand name still attached itself to scooters a few years later in the form of attractive single seater sidecars known as the Sprite, Swift and the Avonette. The Swallow Coachbuilding Co (1935) Ltd was eventually sold to the Birmingham sidecar manufacturers Watsonian who continued to use the Swallow name for some time. Approx 2,500 Swallow Gadabouts were sold between November 1946 to September 1951.

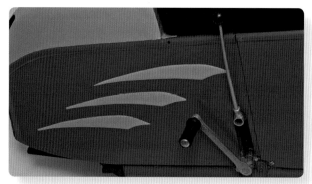

Hand change gearlever above the kickstart.

Following on from the Gadabout Frank Rainbow designed and built a second scooter in 1950 which he named Joyrider. It was a lightweight machine with the lines of a 'step-through' made famous by the Japanese ten years later. It featured a 98cc Villiers engine with a two speed gearbox, large spoked wheels, legshields and a large single seat. The engine was positioned between the rider's legs with a smart top enclosure, however scooter type footboards were not provided only motorcycle footrests. Unfortunately the Joyrider remained as a prototype, but it was used for sometime by Mrs Rainbow and still exists today.

Following the disappointment of the Joyrider scooter came a highlight for Frank Rainbow with the design and construction of a sports car for the hungry American market.

The first car – based on the mechanical components of the Triumph TR2 and called a Doretti – was delivered to America in September 1953 just nine months from conception.

TECHNICAL DATA

YEAR	1948
ENGINE	122cc Villiers 9D
GEARBOX	3 speed car type hand change (MKII foot change)
SUSPENSION	MKI none; MKII front leading link
POWER	4 bhp
TOP SPEED	35 mph
COST (1949)	£103.1.10
CONDITION	Repainted

The car sold well and a second model, the Sabre, was in prototype form when political problems brought production to a halt in 1955, 275 Doretti cars were produced and incredibly nearly 180 are known to survive today.

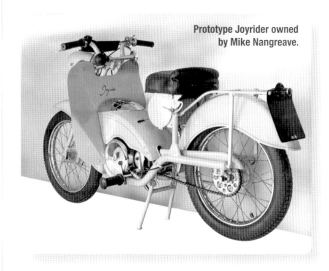

Prototype Joyrider owned by Mike Nangreave.

The Gadabout in the collection is a 1948 MK I in complete and fair condition – it has not been modified with the fan cooling – although made in 1948 the machine was not registered until August 1950.

The powerful Swallow Doretti, designed by Frank Rainbow, owned by Mike Nangreave.

BROCKHOUSE CORGI 1947-54

'The total weight of the machine is 95 lbs and it can be taken upstairs if you so desired.' 'After opening up the machine and giving it a good shaking… it is ready for starting.'

These are words from the Corgi brochure. The advertising also stated 'Low in price, Low in upkeep, High in performance.' But the Corgi handbook contradicted the high performance a little by warning 'this machine should not be run at speeds exceeding 30 mph.'

The Corgi was a lightweight scooter announced in 1946 and finally available to the public in Britain at the beginning of 1948. It was designed by an engineering research company set up after World War Two servicing the motor industry and was manufactured by Brockhouse Engineering (Southport) Ltd. The engineering research company was run by John Dolphin. (The Corgi was based on the military paratroopers scooter known as a Welbike produced

The likeness can be seen.

during the war at the Special Operations Executive at Welwyn under the direction of Lieutenant – Colonel John R.V.Dolphin.) The name chosen for this tiny post war machine was Corgi reflecting the dog of the same name with its little legs and long body.

During the war years Dolphin had come into contact with the Managing Director of Brockhouse Engineering who was looking for a workload to replace military contracts. Soon agreement was reached for the Motor Cycle Division of Brockhouse to manufacture the Corgi scooter.

The open post-war roads for a lucky Corgi.

Design changes were obviously necessary to the Welbike to meet Construction and Use Regulations and remove any restriction imposed by the War Department for fitting into a parachute drop canister. Therefore the pressurised tank was replaced with a gravity feed saddle tank, a mudguard and a 4" front brake was fitted along with an enclosure over the rear wheel to protect the rider. The engine chosen was the 98cc Excelsior Spryt with single speed as used in their Autocycle, this would be made under licence by Brockhouse. In the early stages the

Welbike's spoked wheels and the paddle start were retained along with the collapsible seat stem, but a new design was used for the folding handlebars. The frame was improved and modified for a centre stand and the rear enclosure. Magneto dynamo lighting, a bulb horn and a more comfortable seat completed the new package. The Corgi had a tank capacity of 1¼ gallons giving a range of about 150 miles at a recommended top speed of 30 mph.

A 30 mph District Nurse, VMCC archives.

A prototype Corgi was first announced in the 'Motor Cycling' magazine in March 1946 and production started in early 1947. Unfortunately the scooter could not be purchased in Britain until the next year as initial numbers went abroad to assist with the Country's poor balance of payments. In fact in 1946 an exhibition 'Britain Can Make It' was held by the Council of Industrial Design at the empty Victoria and Albert Museum, all the design items on show – including clothes, furniture and even a futuristic electric bicycle – could only be sold abroad. (The exhibition was given the nick name 'Britain Can't have It' by the Press). Therefore those wishing to buy one of the first Corgis had a lot in common with the many people who attended the show but couldn't buy a thing!

Brockhouse claimed by March 1947 that Corgis were being sold in 48 countries with the USA taking a high output. By March 1948 they were available on the home market at a cost of £66-0-10, the sole concessionaires and the main dealer was Jack Oldings & Co Ltd of Mayfair a company known for dealing in quality motor cars including Rolls-Royces. At this time due to weaknesses with the spoked wheels they were gradually replaced with disc wheels and in July 1948 the MK II was announced with a kick start version of the Excelsior engine.

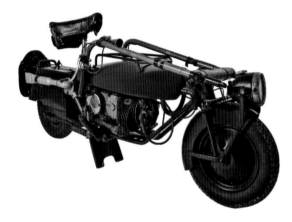

As soon as the Corgis hit the roads in Britain the accessories started to become available, carriers for shopping and office trips together with pannier bags and baskets, a screen for weather protection and a speedo to make sure 30 mph was not exceeded.

Soon the Corgi MK III including a two speed gearbox and a hinged rear mudguard to assist wheel changing was available, and then in November 1951 the MK IV was announced with front suspension, the two speed gearbox and a carrier on top of the tank. Furthermore, the saddle and footrests were increased in size and a metal shield was fitted at the front giving the scooter protective legshields. Also, a larger headlamp was positioned near the top of the legshields and an electric horn above the front wheel – this arrangement still allowed the handlebars and shield to be folding down in one piece.

The ultimate accessory was a full body conversion kit sold by J Olding and Co. Ltd. – this encased the whole machine giving the scooter legshields, footboards and

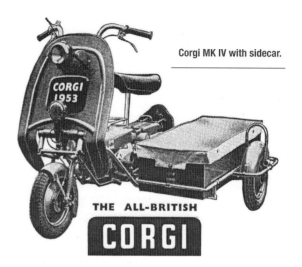

Corgi MK IV with sidecar.

THE ALL-BRITISH
CORGI

a small boot at the rear, the price was 11 guineas plus fitting which included repositioning the fuel tank. It was not long before the tiny Corgi was being asked to pull a sidecar for shopping loads and carry items for the small trader. The first sidecar came in July 1948 and by 1949 a banking sidecar was available from K.V.P. Motors Ltd, London, at a price of £18-18-0.

Corgi 'firsts' included Club weekend ride-outs and endurance tests – these activities would soon be very popular with all scooter clubs during the scooter boom of the mid 1950s. It is estimated that 27,000 Corgis were produced between 1947 and 1954.

The Corgi in the collection is a restored Mk II with the kick-start but has been fitted with a MK IV tank and carrier.

TECHNICAL DATA

YEAR	1948 MKII
ENGINE	98cc Excelsior Spryt
GEARBOX	1, (MK III 2) speed
SUSPENSION	Rigid, (MK IV front telescopic)
POWER	2 bhp
TOP SPEED	30 mph
COST (1948)	£66.0.10
CONDITION	Restored

BOND MINIBYKE 1950-53

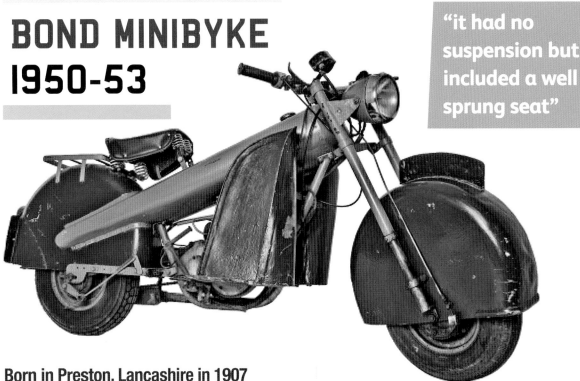

"it had no suspension but included a well sprung seat"

Born in Preston, Lancashire in 1907 Lawrie Bond served an engineering apprenticeship followed by work in the drawing office at Meadows Engineering Ltd in Wolverhampton. He then moved onto a position with the Blackburn Aircraft Company where he gained his experience in the design and materials relating to lightweight aircraft.

In 1944 he set up his own small engineering company to undertake the manufacturer of vehicle and aircraft components for Government Contracts. After the war he moved his Bond Aircraft and Engineering Company to Longridge, Lancashire to pursue his interest in the design of vehicles and engines.

With the lack of materials and money in the late 1940s, a new small racing car – having maximum excitement for minimum cost – soon became popular and the class for 500cc racing cars was born. In June 1947 at a hill climb in Worcestershire a small yellow car, known as the Doodlebug, designed and driven by Bond appeared as a challenger – he then went on to win the Jersey Bouley Bay hill climb in the July.

The 500cc class soon became very competitive, the leading manufacturer was the father and son team of Charles and John Cooper. One of the competitors who drove a Cooper was Alvin 'Spike' Rhiando who went on to ride his own scooter to the

An attractive picture from the brochure showing the telescopic forks.

Sahara and design the Harper Scootomobile a few years later. Strong competition for the winning Coopers were cars designed by Cyril Kieft who later would import the expensive German Hercules scooter and design his own DKR scooters.

In 1949, one year after the introduction of the Bond Minicar, Lawrie Bond announced his Bond Minibyke at the London Earls Court Show. The design was radical, it was half motorcycle half scooter with small covered wheels, footboards and legshields but lacked the scooter step through facility.

A late 1940's Bond Minicar MK A.

It showed Bond's aircraft background with a riveted aluminium tapered oval frame from headstock to rear mudguard with the engine hanging from this main member on 1" x ¼" steel strips – it had no suspension but included a well sprung seat and 4.00 x 8in. tyres. The engine used was the 98cc Villiers which was joined a few months later by a 125cc JAP (J.A.Prestwick) engine in the deluxe model.

Due to a number of front fork failures the solid forks were replaced in April 1950 with telescopic forks and in May 1950 the manufacturing rights for the

Bond Minibyke were sold to Ellis (Leeds) Ltd. of Leeds who replaced the engine mounting strips with a more robust tubular frame. Due to the short supply of the 125cc JAP engines the majority of Minibykes sold were the standard model with the 98cc Villiers. Production ended in July 1953 but not before a total of 750 had been made, the majority – approximately 600 – by Ellis.

The Minibyke in the collection has the 98cc Villiers engine and was produced in 1951 by Ellis having the tubular engine frame. The machine is complete and in fair condition with a new seat.

TECHNICAL DATA

YEAR	1951
ENGINE	98cc Villiers 9D
GEARBOX	2 speed hand change (deluxe – JAP 3 speed)
SUSPENSION	Rigid, then telescopic
POWER	2.8 bhp
TOP SPEED	35 mph
COST (1950)	£69.17.0
CONDITION	Tidy

THE BRITISH AUTOCYCLE

The British Autocycle was developed following the Budget in 1931 when the road tax licence for motorcycles less than 150cc was reduced to fifteen shillings. From 1934 onwards manufacturers began to produce lightweight machines on strengthened bicycle frames with a 98cc engine and single speed gearbox that could be given pedal assistance on steep hills.

During World War Two a number of companies including James and Rudge were allowed to continue Autocycle production for civilians undertaking war work such as air wardens and district nurses.

Villiers had introduced their 98cc Junior engine before the war and this became the most popular engine for this type of machine. A near standard design for the Autocycle developed with the engine at bottom bracket position, the tank between the upper and lower down tubes and side covers over the engine. Also, the norm was a single speed transmission with no suspension.

Young lady enjoying her Autocycle.

BSA made a prototype Autocycle in the late 1930s with a rounded tank and the looks of a lightweight motorcycle – but it never reached production. Also in 1950 Motor Cycling magazine tested a handsome Italian Motom Autocycle with a 48cc four-stroke engine, three speed gearbox and a modern pressed steel frame. Motom were looking for a British company to make the machine under licence – no one was interested. One or both of these machines may have put new life into the British Autocycle scene.

The attractive Motom Autocycle with a four-stroke engine, unfortunately no one was interested.

Villiers improved their 98cc engine over the life of the Autocycle from Junior to Junior De Luxe and in the later years the Mark 2F which produced 2 bhp @ 3,750 rpm but still only had a single speed. A number of Autocycles manufacturers went on to produce scooters later in the 1950s including Excelsior, James, Sun and Dayton.

The last Autocycle on the market was the New Hudson 'Re-styled' that lasted until 1958, it was called Re-styled as the metal covers stretched from the tank over the engine and back to the rear wheel

hub. In 1957 the price of the Restyled was £75.12.0 when a smart 49cc NSU Quickly de-luxe moped with two speeds cost just £69.19.0.

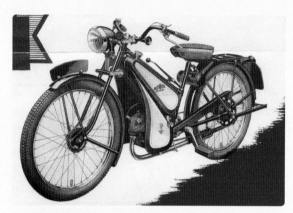

1950 Excelsior Model G2 Autocycle.

By 1957 Continental mopeds were flooding the British market, some with three speed gearboxes and dual seats, many in bright colours, all faster and more attractive than the 98cc Autocycle. The British Autocycle did a good job as a utilitarian lightweight machine and even helped the women's liberation movement during the war but the machine looked like a 1920's design that should never have lasted through to the late 1950s.

The Autocycle and scooter helped with women's liberation.

DOUGLAS VESPA 1951-65

"By March 1951 the first Douglas Vespas were available"

The British Douglas Motorcycle Company began building their flat twin motorcycles in 1907, after World War Two the company announced their new 350cc flat twin known as the T35 and in 1955 this was updated and named the Dragonfly.

In 1955 the company was taken over by Westinghouse Brake and Signal Company Limited and by March 1957 all motorcycle production at their works in Kingswood, Bristol ceased.

In Italy the Piaggio family business was started in 1884 and progressed from a sawmill into ship fitters and builders of railway carriages and aeroplanes. During World War Two Enrico Piaggio was in charge and the companies war efforts included the manufacture of bomber aircraft.

The 2L2 model showing the rod operated gear change.

The companies large factory at Pontedera was very badly damaged due to RAF bombing in 1944 and plans to rebuild ran parallel with continuing their past transport theme and building a new motor scooter.

The job was given to Corradino D'Ascanio an aircraft engineer and inventor of the helicopter. After just months of design and drawing the first Vespa scooter was shown to the Press in 1946 and initial production started straight away. The scooter had a monocoque body with the engine and other components bolted to this shell, the engine was just 98cc and the scooter was sold with a single seat. The engine size was soon increased to 125cc so a passenger could be carried.

In 1948 the Douglas Motorcycle Company had the Receivers in and at this time the Managing Director Claude McCormack while on holiday in Italy

saw the new Vespa scooter on the road. On his return discussions took place with Piaggio and an agreement was reached to make the Vespa under licence at the Douglas works in Bristol. The scooter was shown on the Douglas stand at the 1949 London Earls Court show and orders were taken. In 1950 it was reported approximately 50 Vespas were imported from Italy and mostly sold in car showrooms – including a Rolls-Royce dealer – due to the initial reluctance of motorcycle dealers to handle the new small machine.

By March 1951 the first Douglas built Vespas, using a number of British components, left the factory gates. The model was the 125cc 2L2 known affectionately as the Rod model due to the small diameter rods used to operate the gear change, the only difference in design necessary for the British market was to move the front headlight from the top of the mudguard to the legshields due to the height requirement under the Construction and Use Regulations.

In 1953 a new G model was produced with a cable gear change instead of the rods and by this time the number of dealers in Britain had increased to 350. The GL2 was introduced in 1954 having a new engine giving an increased brake horsepower. Since the start of production in 1951 Douglas were producing an earlier model to the one being made by Piaggio in Italy, however, in 1955 when Douglas was taken over by Westinghouse production improved and the current model was made in Britain.

Throughout the production years at Bristol the company never produced as many Vespas as Piaggio wanted for the British and Commonwealth market and as time went on the number of parts for the scooter made in Italy increased.

The Vespa GS 150 sport machine was always an Italian import, however in 1961 a 150cc Sportique was made by Douglas.

side panels and front mudguard. The 'Douglas Vespa' badge was never used on production models – it was after all a Piaggio Vespa made under licence by Douglas. However, the Douglas name did feature on some of the cast components made at the Bristol works.

Have I passed the Test on my new Vespa?

The 125cc model continued to be updated until 1965 when Douglas ceased production and became an importer of the Italian made Vespas. In 1982 imports were taken over by Vespa (UK) Ltd. part of the Heron Suzuki Group which had developed from the old Lambretta Concessionaires.

This arrangement lasted until 1992 when Piaggio took control of their own imports to Britain. It is estimated that approximately 125,000 Vespas were made by Douglas from 1951 to 1965.

The Douglas Vespa in the collection is an early 1951 Rod model and it is one of the first 100 or so scooters with aluminium

She loves me she loves my Vespa.

TECHNICAL DATA

YEAR	1951
ENGINE	125cc
GEARBOX	3 speed hand change
SUSPENSION	front – trailing link rear – pivoted arms
POWER	4.5 bhp @4,500 rpm
TOP SPEED	43 mph
COST (1952)	£120.16.0
CONDITION	Fully restored

BAC GAZELLE 1952-53

"the only British scooter at the 1951 London show"

Following on from the Bond Minibyke Lawrie Bond's company the Bond Aircraft and Engineering Company produced a very small motorcycle known as the BAC Lilliput made in small numbers until 1952. At the 1951 London Earls Court Show Bond announced the small BAC Gazelle scooter – the only British scooter at the show.

It followed conventional scooter design with a step through frame and small 4.00 x 8in tyres, a duplex frame came down from the headstock and, as with the Swallow Gadabout, used the two frame members as exhaust pipes. It had telescopic front forks and a hoop frame that supported a single seat and a petrol tank above the rear mudguard. Instead

No rear bodywork, just six metal strips to protect the rider from the hot engine.

Very rare Gazelle 125cc with sidecar.

of rear bodywork the Gazelle had just a metal strip cage to keep the riders clothes off the hot engine, a later design for this 'cage' consisted of six 1 ¾" wide metal strips which slightly improved the looks.

Originally the rear tank looked to be specifically designed for the Gazelle, but later models used tanks from the Lilliput motorcycles.

The first Gazelles used the 125cc Villiers 10D engine but later in October 1952 a 98cc machine was made available, at least one 125cc model was made with a sidecar. The price of the 98cc was £94 and £107-10s for the 125cc model. Unfortunately the scooter was not a success – it was unattractive and the turning circle was extremely poor as the forks too readily came into contact with the legshields. Manufacturing ceased in 1953 and production figures were small.

In late 1952 the design of the scooter was sold onto Projects and Developments Ltd, Blackburn, Lancashire. This company of consulting engineers proposed a few modifications moving the petrol tank above the engine and making room for a passenger seat but no more was heard of it. One of Bond's staff was recruited to work for Projects and Developments to design another scooter which was shown at the 1953 Earls Court Show called the Oscar.

And finally at the 1955 Earls Court Show in the exhibitor's car park Lawrie Bond showed his Sherpa scooter. This was another 98cc Villiers engine machine with two speeds, front and rear suspension, a glass-fibre body and a weight of just 123lbs. Although the body material was advanced for the time it was probable the dated look around the handlebars and headlamp plus the two speed gearbox which stopped its progress. Only one prototype machine is thought to have been made – however, this was not the last time the Bond name would be seen on a glass-fibre bodied scooter.

TECHNICAL DATA

YEAR	1953
ENGINE	98cc Villiers
GEARBOX	2 speed hand change
SUSPENSION	front – telescopic rear – rigid
POWER	2.8 bhp @ 4,000 rpm
TOP SPEED	35 mph
COST (1952)	£94
CONDITION	Original – fair

Bond Sherpa prototype with glass-fibre bodywork.

The Gazelle in the collection is a 1953 model with the 98cc Villiers engine first registered in Leicester on the 5th July. It is complete and in fair condition and believed to be the only example to survive.

TANDON STARLETT 1954

> "a Starlett scooterette was on the Tandon stand"

Devdutt Tandon started building inexpensive British lightweight motorcycles in 1948 for the home and export market. His first motorcycle had a Villiers 122cc engine with a three speed gearbox and telescopic front forks.

Tandon
INTRODUCING
1953 MODELS

All frames are made of "KROMO" Accles & Pollock Tube

125 c.c. IMP

The range of machines was increased over the next few years to include a 197cc model, a scrambler and eventually a 322cc Anzani engine motorcycle.

At the 1954 London Earls Court Show a Starlett Scooterette was on the Tandon stand with the Tandon name on the tank, this was a pleasant looking fully enclosed machine with legshields and footboards and large diameter spoked wheels. It was a modern looking machine for Autocycle man and especially for Autocycle woman as the engine was provided with a hand start. The Scooterette was not made by Tandon but made by the French motorcycle manufacturer Monet-Goyon with a 98cc Villiers engine.

The January 1955 Power and Pedal Magazine stated 'A late comer slipped into Earls Court at the last moment, then made quite a hit with the crowds. It is a pretty 98cc scooter from the famous French firm of Monet-Goyon and called the Starlett.'

The fan cooled engine with a two speed gearbox was fitted with a hand starter lever, front suspension was by Gregoire and the steel body provided total enclosure and good weather protection. The machine was available in either green or yellow and priced at £115 .

Monet-Goyon was no stranger to scooters having produced their first one in 1919 using a British Wall Moto-Wheel engine and an attractive wicker seat – the machine needed a paddle start like the first Corgis. Also Monet-Goyon was no stranger to Villiers engines as the company made the units under licence from the 1930s. As Tandon never went ahead to import the Starlett (produced from 1953 to 1957) it can only be assumed that the reaction at the show was not such a hit or the negotiations with Monet-Goyon were not a success. A shame because it would have filled a gap in the scooter market at the time and, if successful, may have assisted Tandon's financial problems in the mid 1950s. However, it has been reported since that Monet-Goyon had many

The hand start for the 98cc Villiers engine.

No wonder the Starlett did not sell at the London Show in November, Brrr.

warranty claims on the Starlett due to weak front forks and thin body panels. So, it looks like Mr Tandon made the right decision about this proposed scooter project.

The French Starlett in the collection has been restored and was purchased via a dealer in Belgium – it has 9590 kilometres on the clock and is a fine example of this attractive looking scooterette.

TECHNICAL DATA

YEAR	1954
ENGINE	98cc Villiers hand start
GEARBOX	2 speed hand change
SUSPENSION	front – Gregoire rear – rigid
POWER	2.8 bhp @ 4,000 rpm
TOP SPEED	40 mph
COST (1955)	£115 (not sold in Britain)
CONDITION	restored

BRITAX SCOOTERETTE 1955-56

"just like a car – overhead valve engine and easy to clean"

The Italian Ducati company was founded by the three Ducati brothers in 1926 and manufactured many items including radios, mechanical calculators and inter-office communications. Their war effort included field radios and other components for the Italian Armed Forces. Following the war and a total factory re-build due to heavy bombing, Ducati negotiated a licence with the engineering company SIATA to build a small 'micromotore' for attachment to bicycles.

The little engine was called Cucciolo (little pup) as the engine noise was similar to a barking puppy, full production started in 1946 and the Cucciolo was an immediate success in Italy.

The suberb Cucciolo engine in a Britax Bike at the Bristol Show 2008.

By 1950 the London based motor and motorcycle accessory company Britax started to sell the 'little pup' into a market already full of cyclemotors. Britax advertisements stated 'a miracle of compact precision engineering' and 'the greatest, speediest, and most flexible small engine ever produced.' And so it was. The Cucciolo was a 48cc four-stroke overhead valve engine with a clutch, two speed gearbox and direct drive to the rear wheel.

It was positioned at the bottom bracket between the pedals, developed 1.25 bhp at 5,250 rpm and promised a performance of 30 mph with 300 mpg. There was a snag – the price was £40 – whereas many cyclemotors could be bought for about £20, but most of these were mounted above the bicycle wheel and had a roller drive from a sometimes crude two-stroke engine. However, it was not long before the cyclemotorist found out the Cucciolo was utterly

reliable, and with its two-speed gearbox on a three speed bike gave a machine with six speeds capable of 40 mph. So, well worth the extra expense.

It did not take long for Britax to realise what a little gem they were importing and that a stronger frame with improved braking was necessary to gain the full benefits from the 'miracle' motor. With the help of Royal Enfield (manufacturers of bicycles and motorcycles) a strengthened bicycle frame with pressed girder forks, 4" diameter drum brakes and balloon tyres was soon available to tame the 'little pup'. A road test in Power and Pedal magazine in

January 1954 gave the Britax bike full marks for its brakes and quoted cruising speeds of 35-42 mph with downhill speeds of 50 mph! The complete special bike and engine was available from late 1953 for a total cost, including tax, of £61-8-6.

Following on from the complete bike Britax announced in late 1954 their Scooterette and Hurricane – both using the Cucciolo engine and the same frame.

The Hurricane was a tiny racing bike with full front fairing, a tuned engine, uprated carburettor and megaphone exhaust. This gave the racer a top speed of over 50mph and it was the machine that aroused interest and started the official class of 50cc racing in Britain.

The scooterette had a welded tubular open frame, rigid rear suspension and front forks of the link type riding on spoked wheels with 20" x 2½" balloon tyres. It had a pressed steel bodywork – giving full protection for the rider – which included a single seat with parcel space under and a rear carrier. A

top speed of 35 mph was quoted in the road tests with a fuel consumption of 180 mpg. Although sold in a high gloss deep maroon with chrome trim it was not an attractive machine. The brochure also stated the Britax Scooterette was just like a car – overhead valve engine, weather protection and easy to clean – the Motorcycling magazine report praised the road holding and excellent centre stand but disliked the limited steering lock.

The magazine may have been exaggerating a little when it quoted the Britax Scooterette was a major attraction at the 1954 London Earls Court Show and saying it was attractively styled, but it was one of only a few British scooters and scooterettes available at the time and it did have that miracle engine. The Scooterette was also reviewed by the Power and Pedal magazine in December 1954 and was the machine that encouraged the magazine to report on scooters in addition to Autocycles and cyclemotors. The January 1955 magazine boasted a new title page entitled Power and Pedal incorporating the Scooter. Sold from November 1954 to August 1956 in limited numbers the Scooterette cost £99-18s. Only a few are known to survive.

In 1954 Ducati sold 40,000 Cucciolos and a further 30,000 lightweight motorcycles – manufacture of the little engine came to an end in 1956. Britax went on to sell motor accessories including seat belts and Ducati went on to win races and produce ever larger motorcycles – from little pups large superbikes grow.

The Scooterette in the collection is thought to be a 1955 model. Unfortunately it has no history or paperwork but is complete and very rare. It is in a fair/repainted condition, the Scooterette script on the legshield is not the original.

TECHNICAL DATA

YEAR	1955
ENGINE	48cc Ducati four-stroke
GEARBOX	2 speed hand change
SUSPENSION	front – link type rear – rigid
POWER	1.35 bhp @ 5,130 rpm
TOP SPEED	35 mph
COST (1955)	£99.18.0
CONDITION	fair – repainted

THE CYCLEMOTOR

The cyclemotor or auxiliary engine fitted to a bicycle type frame existed right at the start of motorcycling, but the boom years were after World War Two when there was a desperate need for personal transport. Little engines were available to fit over the rear or front wheel of a bicycle, at bottom bracket position between the pedals and also built into the rear wheel. The drive from engine to wheel varied from a roller driving the tyre to a belt or chain driving one of the bicycle wheels.

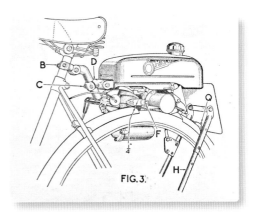

From the Mini-Motor Instruction Book – fitting your cyclemotor.

Prices ranged from £40 plus for the Ducati Cucciolo (known as the 'miracle motor') down to below £20 for a single speed two-stroke unit driving the tyre by roller. The size of the engines ranged from a tiny 18cc to the normal maximum capacity of 49cc.

The Trojan Mini Motor with horizontal cylinder.

One of the first auxiliary engines was a small industrial unit designed by the Italian Vincenti Piatti (later to design the Piatti scooter) called the Mini-Motor and produced by Trojan Ltd of Croydon, Surrey. The motor was a 49.9cc, single speed and clutchless and mounted over the rear wheel with roller drive to the tyre. Production started in 1949 and it soon became one of the most popular cyclemotors at a cost of £21 in the early 1950s. The Mini-Motor was improved by Trojan over the production period and a larger unit of 75cc used for commercial tricycles, however, by the mid 1950s an improved type of personal transport was being demanded and Trojan ceased production in 1956 having made more than 70,000 units. Trojan apprentices made a number of small scale Mini-Motors (not operational) to assist with sales, one of these in its travelling box (and a Trojan 200 Bubble car) can be seen in the Croydon Museum www. museumofcroydon.com.

Another popular cyclemotor positioned over the rear wheel and driving by roller was the Power Pak – the standard model without a clutch was sold alongside the 'Synchromatic Drive' model, this deluxe model cost 26 Guineas and allowed the rider to control the clutch and speed using the handlebar twist grip. The Power Pak was an all British design and was sold from 1950 to 1956.

100,000

Cyclemaster is the original and best motor-wheel, tried and tested by more than 100,000 users in this country alone—and by many others overseas. We receive many such letters as "My Cyclemaster has travelled over 30,000 miles and is still giving excellent service."

Cyclemaster is completely self-contained and it fits any bicycle or tandem. The drive is by enclosed chains so that there is no risk of power slip and no roller to wear the tyres. A clutch enables you to keep the engine running in traffic, and a powerful back-pedalling brake and lighting dynamo are included in price.

£27 - 10 - 0   **EASY TERMS**
Price includes special wheel, tyre, back-pedalling brake, lighting dynamo and six months guarantee

230 M.P.G.   **20 M.P.H.**

Cyclemaster

CYCLEMASTER LIMITED (Dept.T.16)
38a ST. GEORGE'S DRIVE, VICTORIA, LONDON, S.W.1

The cyclemotor that had the most successful sales in Britain was the Cyclemaster, the unit originated from Holland based on a pre-war German design. It was a very clever design housed within the bicycle rear wheel and having the narrow width to fit within the standard bicycle rear forks. Within the unit was the 25.7cc engine, transmission, magneto, tank and exhaust all housed in a 12 ½" diameter shell. The Cyclemaster was announced in September 1950 by Cyclemaster of South Kensington, London and made by EMI at Hayes, Middlesex, the unit sold for £25 including fitting and very soon became known as the 'Magic Wheel'. In 1952 the engine size was increased to 32cc and was reported to give the performance of the normal 49cc units. Also in 1952 a special strengthened frame with just a front wheel and front brake (by this time the Cyclemaster included its own rear brake) was made for the unit by Mercury Industries of Birmingham manufacturers of bicycles.

This was Mercury's first step into the motorised world which was followed in 1956 with both a moped and a small scooter called the Hermes.

By September 1954 100,000 Cyclemasters had been sold but at that time more Autocycles were entering the market so Cyclemaster announced the Cyclemate, this was a frame with hub brakes built by Norman Cycles of Ashford, Kent with the engine positioned just forward of the bottom bracket selling for £48-19-8. It was reported to be 'truly amazing' – but unfortunately for Cyclemaster the German NSU Quickly arrived on the market at the same time – this was really truly amazing, a 49cc German Autocycle with 2 speeds, front suspension and with very attractive lines compared to similar two wheelers of the time all for the price of £59-17-4.

With high numbers of cyclemotors having been sold since 1949 the market started to decline and the budget of 1955 came as a blow to manufacturers when the 25% Purchase Tax was placed on these auxiliary motors bringing the cost of the 'magic wheel' to £33-18-3. Cyclemaster could see the changing scene and announced in 1956 the manufacture of the Piatti scooter designed by Vincenti Piatti. In 1960 the company was bought by Britax and Cyclemaster production ceased with a total of 181,000 units having been made.

In February 1954 the Power and Pedal magazine reported on new two-wheeled registrations for the first nine months of 1953 – 35,164 cyclemotors had been registered against a total figure of 113,631 two-wheelers, one third of new registrations were cyclemotors. For sometime the magazine's editorial had been asking why the British Motorcycle Industry was not supplying this market and also giving them advice on the three 20's rule. The unit should cost less than £20, weigh no more than 20lbs and give a cruising speed of 20mph – the magazine also warned potential makers that they 'must take it seriously.' So Power and Pedal was pleased to announce in June 1954 – on their first visit to BSA's new works at Waverley, Birmingham – the manufacturer of BSA's Winged Wheel 35cc cyclemotor. The magazine was impressed with the quality of the Winged Wheel but mentioned 'the big fellows are a trifle late coming in'. Unfortunately this set the scene for the British Motorcycle Industry (the big fellows) they were also a trifle late entering the expanding moped market and more than a trifle late entering the more profitable scooter market.

At last the British Motorcycle Industry produces a cyclemotor.

During the period 1949 to 1961 over twenty different makes of cyclemotors were available in Britain. The end of the cyclemotor market came in 1961 – the price list for June showed the Cyclemaster and two other units but by December no cyclemotors were listed and the scooter price list was followed by the listing of seven three-wheeled cars confirming the presence of a more demanding and affluent society.

KIEFT R200 1955-56

Technical Representative was the charming Mrs Irene Harris

The Kieft R200 was an imported scooter from Germany, however, the model was very much a part of the British scooter development and history. The Hercules company of Nuremburg built the R200 scooter which was developed in cooperation with TWN (Triumph Werke Nuremburg).

The Hercules R200 was a luxury touring scooter with a tubular frame housing a Sachs 191cc engine with an electric start and four speed gearbox, the final

drive was by chain and the ten inch wheels were interchangeable with split rims. To give the scooter improved balance the two 6v batteries and two interconnecting fuel tanks were housed behind the front legshields. The German scooter could not be sold under the Hercules name as a British Hercules company was already selling bicycles and mopeds.

The scooter, wearing a Kieft badge, was shown at the 1955 London Earls Court Show along with a Hercules moped that the Cyril Kieft Co. Ltd. (Motor Cycle Division) were also importing. Their advertisement for the show stated 'Kieft presents the finest scooter and moped in the world', and showed photographs of the scooter and moped with the words 'Another Kieft Success' printed over a chequered flag and a winning Kieft racing car.

It then reinforced how lucky new owners would be 'Your scooter and moped are backed by the skill and experience of men who have made Kieft Racing cars famous for their unfailing reliability.'

Mrs Irene Harris posed on the Kieft scooter ready for her next visit to the dealers.

But it was not only the Kieft men that were selling the machine the Scooter Sales and Technical Representative was the charming Mrs Irene Harris – skilled in grass track racing on DMW motorcycles – who was out there selling the scooter and explaining the technical bits to the agents and dealers. The Motor Cycling magazine road test in 1955 stated 'The excellence of the brakes and handling characteristics at all speeds were reasons for good marks being attributed to the new Kieft venture.'

Cyril Kieft was a steel industrialist who ran engineering companies in both Bridgend, Wales and the Midlands – he was also a racing driver and a pioneer builder of 500cc class racing cars. His Formula 3 cars were a leading challenge to Coopers dominance and won many races with Stirling Moss at the wheel.

The imported scooter had the Hercules name removed from the front legshields and an attractive enamel shield badge fixed on the front mudguard with the Kieft name and showing the Welsh Dragon similar to the badges worn on his racing cars. Wishing to have a British input to the growing scooter market Mr Kieft's engineers replaced the German Sachs engine with a 197cc Villiers engine with electric start.

The Kieft badge on a 500cc racing car, later used on the scooter.

A Mr Tipper and his young attractive pillion passenger rode the modified machine on a 6,000 mile European trip lasting two months at the end of 1956 to try things out. Everything went fine said Mr Tipper and a Kieft scooter with a 200cc and 150cc Villiers engine appeared in the price list for a few months.

The Villiers Kiefts never went into production – however Mr Kieft had another plan, build a completely British scooter with a Villiers engine but keep an eye on the luxury German Hercules machine when preparing the design drawings. [When Kieft's British scooter was released the Hercules was still sold in Britain named a Prior.]

TECHNICAL DATA

YEAR	1956
ENGINE	191cc
GEARBOX	4 speed foot change
SUSPENSION	Front – leading link Rear – swinging fork
POWER	10.25 bhp @ 5,250 rpm
TOP SPEED	60 mph
COST (1955)	£217
CONDITION	Original – fair

The Kieft with a 150cc engine was shown as £57 cheaper than the R200 with the Sachs.

The Kieft in the collection has had just two family owners and covered 18,000 miles, it is in original condition and was taken off the road in 1965.

The Kieft alongside a maroon and cream Prior Viscount.

DKR DOVE
1957-61

"Housing a triangular petrol tank over the front wheel"

Mr Cyril Kieft was considering building a British scooter in 1955 when BSA announced their Beeza, the thought of this large motorcycle company with their dealer network building a scooter put Mr Kieft's plans on hold.

However, when the Beeza failed to reach production the plan was on again, the first phase was to test Villiers engines in his imported German Hercules scooter (sold as a Kieft) followed by discussions with Willenhall Motor Radiators of Wolverhampton on the final design and manufacture of an all British scooter.

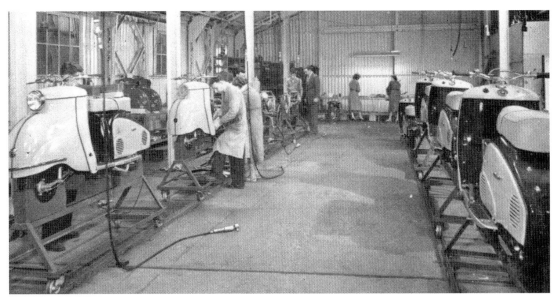

DKR Wolverhampton works with finished scooters on the right.

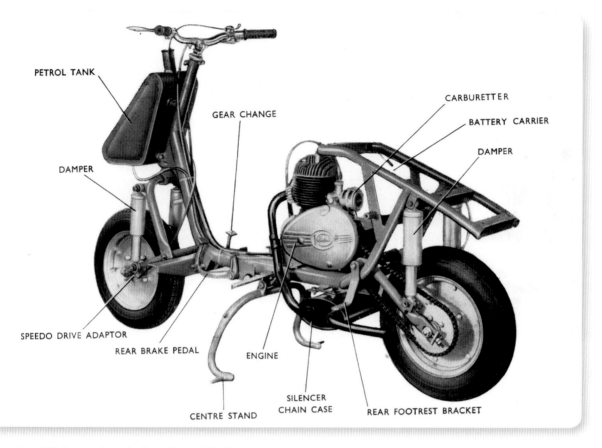

PETROL TANK

GEAR CHANGE

CARBURETTER

BATTERY CARRIER

DAMPER

DAMPER

SPEEDO DRIVE ADAPTOR

REAR BRAKE PEDAL

ENGINE

CENTRE STAND

SILENCER
CHAIN CASE

REAR FOOTREST BRACKET

Diagram from Rider's manual showing forward mounted tank.

DKR takes its name from Mr Kieft and Messrs Day and Robinson Directors of Willenhall, a new company called DKR Scooters Ltd was formed to make the machine.

Cyril Kieft was very proud of the time taken to develop the scooter – five months from drawing board to three scooters on the road in June 1957. The DKR Dove was announced to the Press on the 24th July at Grosvenor House at a price of £162-15-0.

The Dove had a tubular frame housing the Villiers 150cc engine with cooling fan and a three speed gearbox operated by heel and toe pedals. It came with 10 inch wheels and a selection of three different two-tone finishes.

Willenhall Motor Radiators – located on the Pendeford Airport in Wolverhampton (close to the Kieft factory) – would be pressing the steel scooter body, making the silencer and assembling and testing the Dove.

No doubt Willenhall were pleased to obtain this additional scooter workload as the manufacture of their metal lorry cabs was probably in decline. Glass- fibre lorry cabs were introduced in 1955 on some makes and other manufacturers were grouping together to build standard cabs. Willenhall standard cabs were used by BMC and Guy, other lorry makers such as Leyland, Albion and Dodge pooled resources and cab manufacture.

The Power and Pedal magazine of August 1957 stated 'the rear bodywork of the Dove benefited from Teutonic inspirations' thus commenting on the similarity of the DKR's rear end to the German Hercules/Kieft. All road testers gave full marks to the road holding and brakes which reflected Kieft's Formula 3 constructors experience. However, they did not like the high position of the engine and high kick-start pedal or the difficulty in removing the sparking plug, but they praised the compartment behind the legshields for handbags and sandwiches which had a 'door ingeniously arranged to clip flat to provide a little tray' – only one sandwich at a time please!

Will they catch me on my Dayton Albatross twin?

Although the rear bodywork took its design from the Kieft, and the top of the legshields and instrument panel was similar, the front of the Dove was totally different housing a triangular petrol tank over the front wheel which unfortunately threw up comments such as 'a rumbustious, blown out chest' and 'a swollen rounded snout' etc. Overall the scooter went down very well with the Press and the public, and in October 1957 Dove production was stepped up to 300 per month due to a flood of orders.

One way of solving the high kick-start problem (especially difficult for ladies in tight-ish skirts) was to introduce an electric start model. In fact in early 1958 two new models appeared a 150cc electric start Pegasus and – to make good use of the excellent road holding and suspension – a 200cc Defiant. [Hundreds of Defiant fighter aircraft were made at Pendeford during the war by Boulton Paul Aircraft Ltd.] At the end of 1958 the exciting 250cc twin Manx was announced with slightly modified side panels to take the extra width of the larger Villiers engine.

The Dove MkII came along in 1960 with a revised frame to lower the engine giving improved weight distribution and bringing down the height of that kick-start pedal. DKR were now on a roll and in 1961 a brand new model shone out of the darkness.

THE NEW
DKR DE LUXE *Defiant*
200 CC...ELECTRIC STARTER
COMPLETE LUXURY RIDING FOR EVERYON

The DKR in the collection is a fully restored Defiant with the 200cc engine in two-tone green and cream. It has covered just over 14,000 miles and is fitted with non standard flashing indicators.

A very happy customer.

TECHNICAL DATA (DEFIANT)

YEAR	1959
ENGINE	197cc Villiers
GEARBOX	4 speed heel and toe change
SUSPENSION	Front – leading link Rear – swinging fork
POWER	8.4 bhp @ 4,000 rpm
TOP SPEED	60 mph
COST (1959)	£188.1.3
CONDITION	Fully restored

John Green restorer of the DKR Green, job well done.

In Oct.'57 the Dove production was stepped up to 300 per month.

EXCELSIOR HEINKEL 1955-56

"The Excelsior name was fitted above the winged Heinkel badge"

In 1896 the Excelsior bicycle company was one of the first British companies to sell motorcycles, during World War Two they produced the Welbike folding scooter for paratroopers and this was developed after the war and sold as a Corgi by Brockhouse Engineering with an Excelsior engine.

By the mid 1950s they were manufacturing lightweight motorcycles with engine sizes between 98cc and 250cc some with Villiers engines and others with their own engines. At the 1955 London Earls Court Show a special announcement stated they would be selling the German Heinkel Tourist scooter as the Excelsior Heinkel. The 'Excelsior' name was fitted above the winged Heinkel badge on the front of the scooter, it was the most expensive and luxurious scooter on the market at the time.

It was powered by a 174cc Heinkel four-stroke engine with a four speed hand change gearbox, it had an electric start, enclosed chain, 10 inch diameter wheels and storage space under the seat and a small folding luggage rack above the Bosch headlamp.

Extras included a spare wheel, rear carrier and a clock. In October 1955 the Motor Cycling magazine tester said 'The Tourist must approach the ultimate in scooter luxury', the machine was well equipped but the price was £247-7-7 when a Dayton Albatross 225cc was £207-18-0 and a Triumph 500cc Speed-Twin motorcycle just £235! For the £40 over the Albatross cost the Heinkel did offer a four-stroke engine, interchangeable split rim wheels, a 12 volt system with a Siba electric start, cast floor boards, storage and luggage facilities, steering and seat locks, a rear bodywork that could be removed in a few minutes, and it was a scooter designed and produced by aircraft engineers – so well worth the extra.

Obviously not a British scooter but it was the first attempt by the British Excelsior Motor Co. Ltd. to test the scooter market – they would be back.

By the 1956 show the Excelsior name had gone and the Heinkel was being imported by Noble Motors Ltd at a new price of £229-10-0, less than the large German 250cc Maicoletta scooter at £235. Excelsior now had another plan for the scooter market.

[The first Heinkel Tourist scooter was the 101 A-O made in 1953, Excelsior imported the 103 A-O model made between 1955 and 1957. The scooter was made in large numbers and constantly updated until its end in 1965. It was sold in the UK from 1955 for ten years.]

The Excelsior Heinkel in the collection is a 1956 model which has been fully restored in a green and grey, it also has a spare wheel sold as an extra.

TECHNICAL DATA

YEAR	1956
ENGINE	174cc four-stroke
GEARBOX	4 speed hand change
SUSPENSION	Front – telescopic Rear – swinging arm
POWER	9.2 bhp @ 5,500 rpm
TOP SPEED	55 mph
COST (1956)	£247.7.7
CONDITION	Restored in green and grey

EXCELSIOR SKUTABYKE 1957-59

"Spelling of the model name Skutabyke gave a clue"

The first Excelsior scooter in the scooter magazine price lists in 1955/56 was not a British scooter, the second Excelsior machine listed in the scooter price lists in 1957/59 was not even a real scooter. The spelling of the model name Skutabyke gave a clue – it was not a scooter and it was not a normal motorbike, most European countries built this half scooter half motorcycle type machine.

The Skutabyke was first shown at the 1956 London Earls Court Show and Excelsior held a competition with a Skutabyke as the prize asking the public to forecast total attendance throughout the week. So, at least shortly after the show one Excelsior Skutabyke would be on the road.

The Excelsior competition prize at the 1956 London Earls Court Show. Mortons Archive.

The machine was the 98cc two speed Consort motorcycle with complete engine enclosures and full legshields and footboards.

The side enclosures had two small doors, one to access the carburettor and a tool box on the opposite side, it came with a dualseat and coachlines on the tank and the side enclosures. Louvres were built into the enclosures to aid with cooling that were fixed each side of the engine with six wing nuts, the large footboards for rider and passenger were covered in rubber with an alloy edging and the telescopic forks also had nice rubber gaiters. The cost was £94-17-3 against the 98cc DMW Bambi scooter at £99-4-0 and the 98cc Mercury Dolphin scooter at £98-19-10.

Maybe the Excelsior Heinkel scooter – which was too luxurious and expensive to sell in high numbers – and the Excelsior Skutabyke – which was too cheap and Skutabyke-ish to sell in high numbers – were stop gaps until Excelsior could bring a proper scooter to the market.

The Skutabyke in the collection is complete – not many have retained their full enclosures – but unfortunately has had a full green makeover. The wing nuts and dualseat have been replaced but it does have the nice Skutabyke transfers on the sides. The wheels, silencer and handlebars have lost their brightwork to the green paint.

Fully enclosed 98 c.c. Excelsior Skutabyke

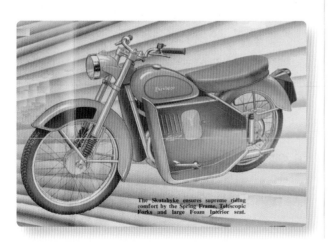

The Skutabyke ensures supreme riding comfort by the Spring Frame, Telescopic Forks and large Foam Interior seat.

TECHNICAL DATA

YEAR	1957
ENGINE	98cc Villiers
GEARBOX	2 speed foot change
SUSPENSION	Front – telescopic Rear – plunger
POWER	2.8 bhp @ 4,000 rpm
TOP SPEED	40 mph
COST (1957)	£94.17.3
CONDITION	a green makeover

SCOOTER MAGAZINES 1950/60s

From the mid 1950s there were a number of magazines publishing information on the growing sales of motor scooters. In the late 1950s three monthly magazines were the most popular source of scooter information – these were Power and Pedal, Scooter World and Scooter & Three Wheeler. Various other publications existed including Practical Scooter and Moped, a weekly magazine called Scooter News, and of course the two main motorcycle magazines The Motor Cycle and Motor Cycling soon had their own scooter sections.

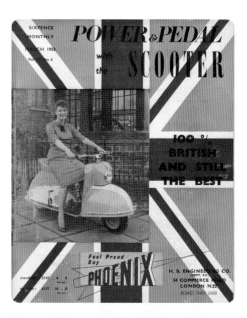

The Power and Pedal magazine was first on the scene in late 1952 to cover the growing sales of cyclemotors (small auxiliary engines) that could be fitted to bicycles. The magazine was published by Power & Pedal Ltd, 197 Temple Chambers, London, its editor was Mr Frank L.Farr and the cost was 4d. As well as the cyclemotor it covered the

British Autocycle and later the European Autocycles (50cc mopeds). So the magazine progressed from calling itself 'The Journal of the Cyclemotor' to 'The Cyclemotor & Autocycle Journal' and then when 50cc scooters came to the market the magazine stated in January 1955 that it incorporated 'The Scooter'.

In the early 1950s Mr Farr repeatedly asked why the British Motorcycle Industry was not making cyclemotors for the three million bicycles on the road and suggesting they apply his 20's rule – a cyclemotor capable of 20 mph, weighing no more than 20lbs. and costing less than £20. This pleading was stressed in the September 1955 magazine for British Makers to satisfy the cyclemotor, Autocycle and lightweight scooter markets. He wanted a British 50cc engine that could be used for all three machines – sadly it was not until the end of the 1950s that Villiers produced their 50cc moped engine which could have satisfied Mr Farr.

By the show number of 1954 the magazine had increased in size and pages, and also increased in cost to 6d. By the 1955 Show number the magazine had dropped the reference to cyclemotors and was now know as 'The Autocycle Journal with the Scooter'. The magazine now adequately covered both the moped and scooter scene and from February 1963 it incorporated 'Three Wheeler News' to retain the readers who had moved on from scooters to bubble cars and three wheelers. The last title change happened in May 1964 when the cover stated 'The Scooter with Power & Pedal' plus 'Three Wheeler News' with a cover price of 9d. The magazine had covered the cyclemotor, the Autocycle, the moped, the scooter boom and three wheelers for a period of twelve years.

A very nice new Bond P4.

The first edition of Scooter World was December 1955, the editor Mr Jon Stevens quoted to his readers 'You have had to wait a long time, but here it is. To coin a phrase, it is of the scooters, by the scooters, for the scooters.' Also he stated 'You, gentle reader , will not have to suffer the sneers of the high-powered gentry, nor the ill-muffled mutterings of the mopeds.' In the magazine it listed the thirteen scooters at the November London Earls Court Show including the 48cc Britax and 49cc Mercury Hermes (mopeds in disguise) and had an advertisement for a Velocette LE motorcycle! The magazine was of the large format, had a bright yellow cover, an office cat and indulged in pretty girls and scooter related cartoons even on the cover, very different from Power and Pedal with its more technical and down to earth approach.

In his editorial in January 1962 Jon Stevens gave a plug for his new book called 'Scootering' and was still lamenting the lack of British Makers in the market. He stated nine out of ten of the half a million scooters on British roads were built abroad, BSA's Chairman had sadly admitted the sales of their BSA Sunbeam/Triumph Tigress scooters had been disappointing and the promise of a British lightweight scooter with no gears made eighteen months ago had still not appeared. However, by March 1962 the new Triumph Tina automatic was announced, unfortunately without being fully developed, so it would be 1965 before the replacement T10 was on the road to satisfy poor Mr Stevens.

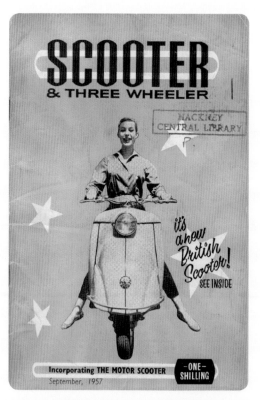

The new DKR Dove scooter with added glamour of course.

In the November 1964 magazine Mr Stevens was again upset about the number of British scooters that had disappeared. He stated 'people will buy scooters. They would buy a British made scooter if one appeared that would lick the imported makes. British firms have all the advantages – except brains and foresight and imagination. Scooters are here to stay. They are part of the scene.' Mr Stevens could rightly see the end of the British scooter and unfortunately the need for a Scooter World magazine.

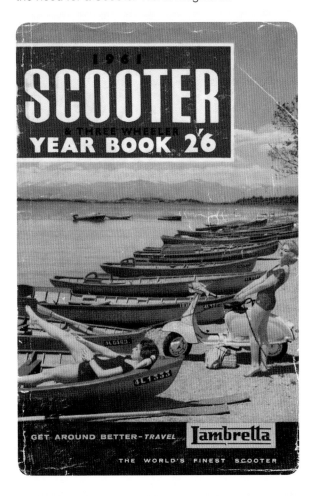

The Scooter and Three Wheeler magazine went on sale in May 1956 at a price of 9d – the editor was Cyril Ayton and the publisher Scooter World Ltd, 8 New Street Square, London, (no association with the magazine Scooter World). The magazine was a small size (5½" x 8½") which made it very handy for reading on the train but meant the text and pictures were also small. In July 1957 the price was increased to one shilling and number of pages increased to over 100. In December 1958 the publisher changed

to Link House who at that time were already publishing numerous magazines including 'Caravan' and 'Exchange and Mart'. The magazine said it wanted to 'bring to those who ride or drive mopeds, scooters and three wheelers a really lively magazine, and which has in fact given us the largest circulation in our field.'

It was a very enjoyable read with a balance coverage of machine reviews and tests, club scene, touring and camping, letters, buyers guides, show reports and of course 'mainly for women'. It stated it was sold in the USA, Canada, Australia, New Zealand and most of Europe. In January 1959 Mr Dennis M Dalton took over as editor and the magazine continued with its winning formula. The magazine also produced a Year Book early in each year – the first 1957 book included reviews of the 1956 road tests, information on the scooter scene on the Continent and in the USA, the history of the scooter, full information on touring and camping and a detailed buyers guide with many pictures. Cyril Ayton said 'In fact we believe this book is rather more – more useful, primarily – than a conventional year book.' It was something special at the time and extremely useful over fifty years later. In the December 1962 buyers guide there were over 20 scooters with an engine of 125cc or above, in January 1966 there were just eight – the end was nigh. The end came in October 1967 – the Scooter and Three Wheeler magazine had given over eleven years of service and enjoyment to those who rode or drove mopeds, scooters and three wheelers.

All three magazines now give extremely useful information to the classic scooter collector and historian, however, to get an accurate account of each machine the letter page with readers good and bad experiences must be read in conjunction with the magazines reviews/road tests. Some of the best scooter road tests were however undertaken by the Motor Cycle and Motorcycling magazines – these followed the same detailed test they use for motorcycles giving a thorough road test, excellent drawings and photographs and a full technical data report.

CYCLEMASTER PIATTI 1956/58

> "the scooter was an unusual design"

The Piatti scooter was designed and developed by the Italian Vincenti Piatti in the early 1950s, Piatti had previously designed the Mini-Motor cyclemotor (made under licence by Trojan of Croydon, Surrey) and also a small folding scooter using the Mini-Motor to drive the rear wheel.

The scooter was an unusual design with the 'works' enclosed in what looked like an upside down bathtub. The engine was 125cc with a 3 speed gearbox, the whole horizontal engine/gearbox unit pivoted with the rear suspension and the final drive.

Introducing THE NEW 125cc. Piatti — The All-British Made Scooter — A CYCLEMASTER PRODUCT

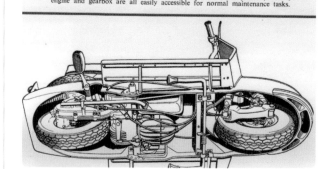

When the machine is laid on its side the front and rear suspension, wheels, engine and gearbox are all easily accessible for normal maintenance tasks.

All other maintenance was undertaken with the scooter on its side.

The new scooter was shown at the Brussels Motorcycle Show in 1952 and made under licence in Belgium from 1954 to 1957, production in Britain began at the end of 1956 and was undertaken by Cyclemaster of Byfleet, Surrey who were still producing the Cyclemaster cyclemotor and an Autocycle.

Only one small door provided an opening in the monocoque body giving access to the petrol tap and carburettor, all other maintenance work – including plug cleaning – was undertaken with the scooter on its side. A small screw was positioned on the petrol tank cap to enable the vent to be closed and prevent leakage. The model was designed to be suitable for ladies with height adjustable handlebars and seat, a large shopping carrier over the front wheel, plus a hand control cable to lower the centre stand.

It has been stated that approximately 800 scooters were made in Belgium and nearly 16,000 in England. There are still a few remaining that delight the collectors due to their quirky design. Most surviving machines show low mileages including the one in the collection which is in original condition with just 3 miles on the clock.

Unfortunately the Piatti had cooling problems and trouble with a few components so although it was priced below a 125cc Vespa and Lambretta its popularity quickly waned.

Advertisements at the time stated the Piatti was sold all over the world and owners affectionately called their little scooter 'Patty'. A minimum cost model came to the market with no front carrier and a simple bicycle type saddle in place of the dualseat/spare wheel, and furthermore a Mk II model with improvements was promised, none of this however stopped production coming to an end in September 1958.

TECHNICAL DATA

YEAR	1958
ENGINE	125cc two-stroke
GEARBOX	3 speed hand change
SUSPENSION	front – leading arm rear – pivots as a unit with engine
POWER	4.7 bhp @ 4,750 rpm
TOP SPEED	41 mph
COST (1958)	£139.10.0
CONDITION	Original – with 3 miles on the clock

MERCURY HERMES 1956

"the machine was designed for short shopping trips"

Strong Mercury bicycle frame for the Cyclemaster at Bristol Motorcycle Show 2010.

Mercury Industries Ltd of Birmingham was set up in 1946 to make bicycles. As a result of an expanding market in both Britain and the USA the company moved to larger premises in Dudley in 1948 with a staff of 200.

The early 1950s was the time of the cyclemotor clip-on unit so Mercury expanded their bicycle range producing a purpose built strong bicycle frame for the Cyclemaster unit that fitted in the rear wheel. Later a pillion seat and footrests were provided for two-up riding on the 32cc engine!

in style . . .

⭐ **A NEW ERA IN TRANSPORT**

THE introduction by Mercury Industries of the "HERMES" Scooter opens up a new era in transport !

The engine, developing two b.h.p. with its ideally selected two-speed gear, will climb any hill and cruise along at a comfortable 25-30 m.p.h. Scientifically balanced, the "HERMES" provides maximum stability, full weather protection and safety under all road conditions. It is easy to keep at home—requires no elaborate garaging and can even be kept in the hall. The Hermes is smartly finished in two tone colour scheme of maroon and grey.

PRICE

£72-10-0

(Plus £16 15s, Tax)

A PRODUCT OF MERCURY INDUSTRIES (BIRMINGHAM) LTD.

The Hermes scooter in the collection is one of the last made in late 1956 and has been fully restored and used on the road in recent years – it is one of approximately ten that have survived. Now as a classic machine it is much admired.

In late 1955 Mercury moved into the real powered two-wheeler business by announcing their Mercette moped and Hermes scooter. The bicycle looking moped was powered by a 48cc Dunkley four-stroke unit and the scooter used a German ILO 49cc two-stroke engine. The Hermes was made under licence and based on the German Meister Solo Roller (single seat scooter). The machine was designed for short shopping trips – especially for the ladies as only a size 8 shoe or less would fit on the flat platform. It was an extremely long scooter with telescopic front forks and a rigid rear end but with a comfortable sprung rubber saddle.

Unfortunately the hand pull start fitted to the German ILO engine was extremely troublesome, however, it is estimated Mercury sold approximately 1100 Hermes scooters between January and November 1956 before the launch of their second machine – a 98cc Dolphin scooter.

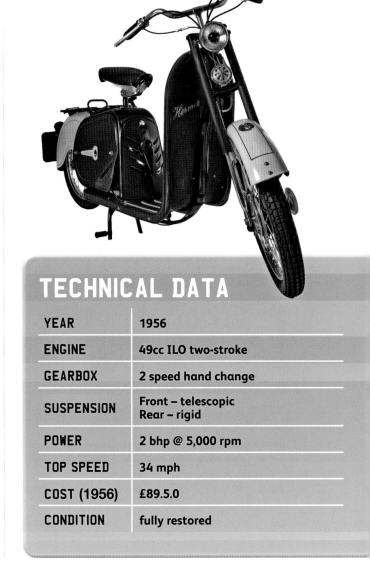

TECHNICAL DATA

YEAR	1956
ENGINE	49cc ILO two-stroke
GEARBOX	2 speed hand change
SUSPENSION	Front – telescopic Rear – rigid
POWER	2 bhp @ 5,000 rpm
TOP SPEED	34 mph
COST (1956)	£89.5.0
CONDITION	fully restored

50

MERCURY DOLPHIN 1957

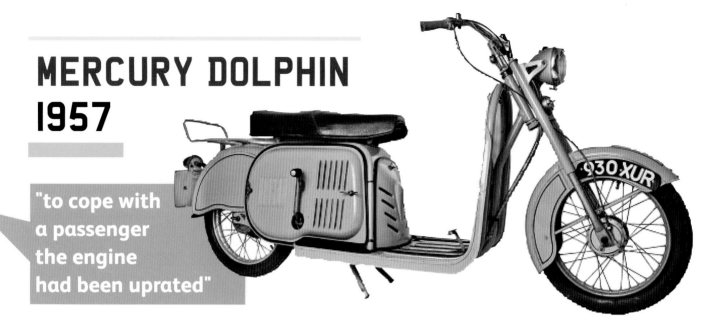

"to cope with a passenger the engine had been uprated"

Production of the Mercury Hermes scooter came to an end in 1956 and at the London Earls Court Show in November the company proudly announced its replacement – the Dolphin. The single sheet flyer stated 'Britain's finest engineering skill and materials combine to produce the sleek, elegant Dolphin scooter'.

So, the Dolphin had arrived for production in 1957, it obviously evolved from the Hermes but was even longer and had a more vertical frame to support a dual seat. To cope with a passenger the engine had been uprated from the 49cc ILO to a 98cc Villiers increasing the power from 2.0 to 2.8bhp, the wheel size had also increased from 15" to 20" diameter.

Just me and my Dolphin cruising the streets.

Shows two speed gear lever and bag hook.

With two up it would have been a little slow on the hills.

Maybe the adverse comments on the looks of the sleek and elegant Dolphin sent Mercury back to the drawing board for a third attempt in 1958. It is thought that less than 10 Mercury Dolphins have survived and not all those are complete, the one in the collection is a fine restored machine and was used regularly by the previous owner.

Obviously the price had also increased by approximately £10 to £98-19-10, but this was very soon raised again to £105-0-0 – still, as the company stated 'You add safety to pleasure when you buy a Dolphin', worth every penny then, plus the ladies were informed that even the daintiest dresses would be protected by the splash proof mudguards. Unfortunately the ride would have been a little hard with the rigid rear end and journeys would have taken a long time with a cruising speed of just 30 mph.

TECHNICAL DATA

YEAR	1957
ENGINE	98cc Villiers
GEARBOX	2 speed hand change
SUSPENSION	front - telescopic rear - rigid
POWER	2 bhp @ 4,000 rpm
TOP SPEED	40 mph
COST (1957)	£98.19.10
CONDITION	restored

MERCURY PIPPIN 1958

"Alas, only about 15 were made"

More time on the Mercury drawing board had been worthwhile as in January 1958 a Champagne Launch at a London Hotel was held to show the new Pippin, 'Three miles for a penny' was the slogan adopted by Mercury Industries Ltd for their new Pippin scooter.

It was stated by management the new machine had already earned $500,000 in orders from the USA – where Mercury had a large market for their bicycles. The Pippin had a similar tubular frame to the ugly Dolphin but had new attractive bodywork, the frame was enclosed in front of the legshields, and the front forks and the handlebars were also covered. The handlebar cover incorporated a hole for a speedo (extra) and places to take a windscreen (extra).

Award winning Pippin at the 2007 Stafford Motorcycle Show.

It's a Pippin

a winner all the way

★ **A Winner in Price –** One of the cheapest British motor scooters on the road.

★ **A Winner On Running Costs –** three miles a penny.

★ **A Winner on Road Ability –** bigger wheels, ideal wheel base, armchair comfort.

★ **A Winner On Performance –** steady 35-40 m.p.h. cruising speed, with 2 up and luggage.

★ **A Winner On Reliability –** thanks to the Villiers 98cc fan cooled engine.

3 miles for a penny— **for only £115-10**
Including Tax

Mercury Industries (Birmingham) · **Sales Office, Hardy House** · **Beak Street** · **London W.1.** · **Telephone GER 4044 /5**

A rare Pippin in the garden.

The wheelbase had been shortened, wheels reduced to 15" diameter and the scooter had smart rear bodywork with a small carrier and a door for the petrol tap. It was a vast improvement in looks over Dolphin but the engine was still the 98cc Villiers with just 2.8 bhp on tap for two up riding. A very attractive model, Julie Alexander, with the compulsory long legs, helped to complete the attractive picture of the new machine. Mercury promised potential owners 35-40 mph, 160 mpg and soon the factory would be producing 15,000 per year. Alas, only about 15 were made before a Creditors meeting in March when the company ceased to exist due to major financial problems.

Most of the parts ready for assembly were sold at auction to a scrap metal dealer for such low prices the auctioneer was heard to mumble 'poor Mercury'.

The Pippin in the collection is number 12 and the only one known to survive – this was found disassembled with a number of bodyparts missing. New parts were made for the handlebar cover, the rear body door and dualseat base all from 1958 small black and white magazine pictures. This rare scooter won 'highly commended' at the 2007 Stafford Classic Bike Show – at last Mercury had got it right, well almost.

TECHNICAL DATA

YEAR	1958
ENGINE	98cc Villiers
GEARBOX	2 speed hand change
SUSPENSION	Front – telescopic Rear – rigid
POWER	2.8 bhp @ 4,000 rpm
TOP SPEED	40 mph
COST (1958)	£115.10.0
CONDITION	Fully restored

EUROPEAN SCOOTERS IN THE EARLY 1950s

Following the introduction and decline of three British scooters (Swallow Gadabout, Corgi and BAC Gazelle) during the period 1946 to 1953 it would be another three years before Dayton, Phoenix and a few other British makes appeared on the market and not until 1958 before a large British Motorcycle manufacturer – the BSA Group – announced their scooter. In Europe things were different.

In Italy Piaggio announced their Vespa in 1946, Innocenti, the Lambretta in 1947 and other smaller companies were already producing scooters at this time. The Italian Motorcycle Industry was quick to follow – MV Agusta had two 125cc scooters for sale in 1949, Moto Guzzi announced their 160cc

The Italian Ducati 175cc automatic electric start super scooter.

Galletto in 1950 and Parilla were selling their Levriere (Greyhound) in 1952 the same year as Ducati announced their advanced 175cc automatic electric start super scooter. Very few of the Italian Motorcycle Industry machines came to Britain apart from a number of Parilla scooters.

Just across the English Channel similar things were happening in France – the scooter industry was kick-started by three companies, Bernardet (a motorcycle side-car manufacturer), AGF, and Mors-Speed between the years 1947 and 1949. Again, the French motorcycle industry followed quickly with Terrot and Motobecane announcing scooters in 1951 and Peugeot and Monet-Goyon in 1953. Approximately 1,200 Terrot scooters were sold in Britain by Phelon and Moore – the Panther Motorcycle Company – and the Peugeot scooters were also available in Britain.

The French Peugeot scooter on tour.

In the early 1950s scooter production also commenced in Germany – in 1950 Lambrettas were made under licence by NSU and similarly Vespas by Hoffman. The same year Strolch introduced a scooter (later to become the Progress) and the Goggo scooter was announced one year later. Also, in 1951 Maico introduced their large fully enclosed Mobil and Bastert

The attractive Austrian Puch scooters were imported for many years.

their expensive de-luxe scooter. Zundapp introduced their popular Bella in 1953 and the first European belt driven automatic scooter, the Hobby, was announced by DKW in 1954. Many of these German scooters were very popular on British roads from the mid 1950s.

Austria's large industrial producer Lohner had their first scooter, the L98, on the road in 1950 and the Austrian Motorcycle manufacturer Puch had their attractive R125 available in 1952. From 1956 CZ/Jawa Motorcycle Company, in the former Czechoslovakia, made their first Cezeta scooter.

In most European countries (including those in the East) many motorcycle manufacturers were moving into the fast expanding scooter market – except one, Britain. All of the scooter magazines in the mid 1950s were constantly asking when the British Motorcycle Industry would produce a scooter to challenge the high European imports. The head of AMC, Associated Motor Cycles Ltd., answered their question with a statement "We shall never make scooters." The British Motorcycle Industry had their problems with old machinery, old motorcycle designs, old Board members, and full order

books for motorbikes so the statement was no surprise – however, he did have to eat his words five years later when AMC announced their James scooter in 1960. It was a British challenge that came too late and did little to worry Piaggio who had announced their millionth Vespa in April 1956.

The German Zundapp Bella scooter was imported by Ambassador Motorcycles.

56

DAYTON ALBATROSS 1956-60

"Dayton had to design a cooling tunnel"

The Dayton story starts way back in 1906 when Mr Charles Day – who had worked in the cycle trade since 1898 – started to sell bicycles under the trade name Dayton. The bicycle trade grew and in 1910 a small range of motorcycles were also developed at their works in Shoreditch, London together with a cyclemotor called the Dayton Cyclet with a 1½hp two-stroke engine.

Dayton continued bicycle manufacture during the 1914-1918 war as well as supplying motorcycles to the British Army. Following the war years the sales of bicycles and motorcycles expanded plus a separate factory was opened to produce wheelchairs for the many war disabled. In 1926 a decision was made to end the manufacture of motorcycles and wheelchairs and concentrate on bicycles at a new factory site at Park Royal, West London.

In 1937 a Mr Frederick Durman joined the company – the same year as the company's name was changed to Dayton Cycle Company Ltd. In 1937 Dayton produced an Autocycle for one year, the price was just 17 guineas – about one guinea

cheaper than most similar machines – very few were made and only one is known to survive today.

Following World War Two Dayton wished to produce a British Scooter to compete with the many continental machines on the road, they decided to go for a machine with a larger engine capacity

NOT ONLY NEW BUT...

the all British Dayton Albatross

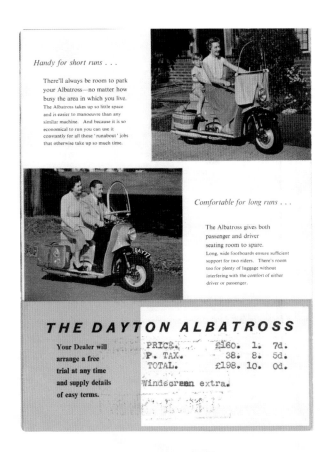

Handy for short runs . . .

There'll always be room to park your Albatross—no matter how busy the area in which you live. The Albatross takes up so little space and is easier to manoeuvre than any similar machine. And because it is so economical to run you can use it constantly for all those 'runabout' jobs that otherwise take up so much time.

Comfortable for long runs . . .

The Albatross gives both passenger and driver seating room to spare. Long, wide footboards ensure sufficient support for two riders. There's room too for plenty of luggage without interfering with the comfort of either driver or passenger.

THE DAYTON ALBATROSS

Your Dealer will arrange a free trial at any time and supply details of easy terms.

PRICE.   £160. 1. 7d.
P. TAX.   38. 8. 5d.
TOTAL.   £198. 10. 0d.

Windscreen extra.

a new model called the Continental having improved curved legshields and front mudguard plus a glove box behind the legshields. However, Mr Durman stated that the British were strange people and did not necessarily like change so the scooter would still be produced with the original style front mudguard and legshields with the Continental rear end. The Dayton Continental twin with its much improved looks, large smooth twin engine, 4.00" x 12" wheels and a top speed of 72 mph was now a truly grand touring scooter.

that would hopefully attract both scooterist and motorcyclists. So, the Villiers MK 1H 225cc engine was chosen, however, no cooling fan was available for the unit so Dayton had to design a cooling tunnel between the rider's legs and shape the front of the machine to allow maximum air flow over the engine. Although shown at the 1954 and 1955 London Earls Court Shows full production of the Albatross did not commence until Autumn 1956. The scooter had good reports on its performance and handling but was criticised for the front design with its straight legshields and totally exposed Earls-type suspension.

In 1957 Dayton announced a second model with the new Villiers 250cc twin engine raising the bhp from 9.6 to 15 and giving a top speed of 72mph. Also the front was improved by incorporating the suspension within a new larger mudguard. A little later a total front revision became available in

Dayton did some advertising for its Albatross but never really produced any sexy or memorable ones. An early advertisement in the Motor Cycle magazine of November 1955 showed a couple on the scooter (grabbed at random from the office?) with a well worn old suitcase strapped to the pannier bag strips at the rear and stating 'higher cruising speeds, greater stability, much more comfort, greater reliability – than any similar machine.'

Dayton 225cc garden shed find with just 3,105 miles covered.

Later in 1958 the advertisement showed a 250cc twin with the wording 'Road Proved'? and 'the only scooter with Motorcycle performance and comfort'. (Maico, Zundapp and BSA may not have agreed).

A very early Albatross showing the fuel tank under the dualseat.

Later the Dayton was mainly featured as one of the many scooters including Bond, Panther, DKR and Phoenix in the Villiers engine advertisements that shouted 'GO BRITISH, GO BY THE BEST BRITISH SCOOTERS AND GO BUY THE BEST BRITISH SCOOTERS WITH VILLIERS ENGINES.'

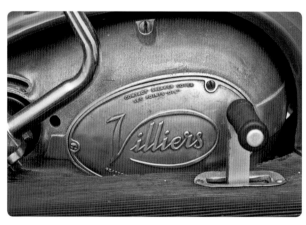

The powerful Villiers 250cc twin engine.

In 1959 Dayton introduced a smaller machine with a 175cc engine called an Albatross Flamenco, this machine was developed in cooperation with the motorcycle companies Panther and Sun. Sales were going well for Dayton with their range of Continental single, Continental twin and the new Flamenco – so

well in fact the company decided to restructure and go for more capital so larger stocks could be held and a new advertising campaign introduced.

Unfortunately this company change spelt disaster for Dayton when they discovered the new holding company M.G.Holdings had used the capital for another company. Dayton closed in 1960 which ended the production of one of the first and one of the best British Scooters.

The blue scooter in the collection is a 1958 Albatross 225cc, it is complete but a shed find and has just 3105 miles on the clock. The red and black scooter is a 1958 Albatross Continental 250cc twin in fully restored condition and a very fine example of this fast touring machine.

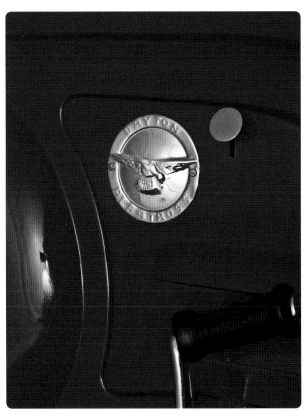

Small side door with Dayton Albatross badge.

TECHNICAL DATA

	225CC	250cc
YEAR	1958	1958
ENGINE	225cc	247cc twin
GEARBOX	4 speed heel and toe	
SUSPENSION	Front – swinging fork Earls type Rear – swinging fork	
POWER	9.6 bhp @ 4,500 rpm	15 bhp @ 5,500 rpm
TOP SPEED	65 mph	72 mph
COST (1958)	£210.10.0	£235
CONDITION	Shed find	Fully restored

PHOENIX
1956-64

"The lines of the scooter were described as having a simple appearance"

Ernie Barrett was a short-circuit and TT motorcycle rider from 1947 to 1957, at times he raced his own motorcycle the Phoenix – JAP using various engine sizes in his own frame so he could race in all three Isle of Man TT classes, this philosophy of one frame and various engine sizes would later be used in his scooter production.

In the very early 1950s he was working on a prototype scooter using both JAP (J.A.Prestwick) and Villiers engines. The first Phoenix scooter was shown at the 1956 London Earls Court Show and production started at his HB Engineering Co. works in Tottenham, London in late 1956. [The name HB came about as Ernie Barrett bought the general engineering and motorcycle company from a Mr Harry Barnes.]

Ernie Barrett with the Phoenix-JAP ridden in the 1953 Junior TT.

An early Phoenix prototype, VMCC archives.

Phoenix employee Bruce Davies – photograph taken by Ernie Barrett.

The Phoenix scooter had a 150cc Villiers engine with a three speed gearbox, front and rear suspension, and rear bodywork retained by three car type bonnet catches. Phoenix advertising stated the three catches made the works 'get-at-able' and reduced maintenance costs, also the scooter's easy to use side stand and two pedal gear change arrangement 'to preserve shoe toe caps' made ideal selling points for the ladies. The lines of the scooter were described in a road test report as having a 'simple appearance' – it certainly was not a good looker.

As purchased before the full restoration.

The Phoenix works at Tottenham had four or five positions to assemble scooters and the plan was to produce about 20 each week. The bodywork, castings and wheels were made by suppliers and HB Engineering made the frames and did the final assembly and testing work. A Motorcycling magazine article mentioned that the company had moved to larger premises at 34 Commerce Road, Wood Green, London, N22, this was obviously in preparation for plans to increase the model range that took place in 1958.

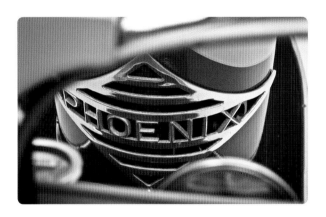

The next 150cc scooter to be announced by Phoenix was the De Luxe model 150 'It's British – It's economical – It's light – It's beautiful – It's roomy' stated the brochure for the new model. 'Simple appearance' to beautiful in just one year!

Certainly bodywork improvements had been made, the headlamp and rear number plate now had attractive metal housings, the large front mudguard was given a more pleasing shape and the rear bodywork had two shapely side panels giving easy access to the carburettor, chain, and cable adjustment without having to remove the whole rear tub. All this for just £10 extra at £157-10s.

In 1958 the range was increased to six machines with engine sizes 150, 200 and 250cc twin, also the metal rear body was replaced with an improved looking glass-fibre tub, still with the 'get-at-able' feature. With six Phoenix models available in mid 1958 a further one was shown at the October London Earls Court show – this was the new T325 with a sidecar fitted.

The T325 used the 250cc twin engine with larger bore cylinders at 325cc, and easily took the title of most powerful scooter available from the 277cc German Maicoletta. The cost for the sidecar outfit was a few pounds under £300,

Laura at the Amberley museum's classic scooter day 2009.

Phoenix proudly showed this scooter at the Villiers Diamond Jubilee Exhibition in Westminster in January 1959. The sidecar was not made by Phoenix.

The plan for the new Commerce Road, Wood Green factory was to increase production from 20 to 100 scooters each week – unfortunately, due to supplier problems this was never achieved and financial problems forced a move in 1959 back to the original Tottenham premises. A name change to 'Phoenix Scooter Company' also occurred at this time. The next improvement to the scooters took place in 1960 with the addition of a more attractive front mudguard and headlamp housing in glass-fibre, also a 175cc was added to the range. In 1961 the legshields were changed to glass-fibre incorporating a larger glove box and full handlebar cowling, the following year the whole scooter became glass-fibre when the metal footboards were re-worked.

Ready for the weekend rally.

THE WORLDS MOST POWERFUL SCOOTER

Super De Luxe Model 325 TWIN

Basic Price £164. 4. 0. Plus P.T. £30. 15. 9.

80 m.p.h. Plus

Superb Road Holding!   80/90 m.p.g.

Terrific Brakes!

IT WILL CRUISE A SIDECAR IN REAL COMFORT AT 50/60 m.p.h. EFFORTLESSLY

The last Phoenix brochure of 1964.

Phoenix 150 at speed.

Three catches made the works 'get-at-able'.

However, by 1962 sales had slowed right down – it has been stated that approximately 3000 Phoenix scooters were made, most during the period 1956 – 1959 and mainly with a 150cc engine. In the final year of production engine sizes ranged from 98 to 325cc, however, the scooters were only made to order. The last 1964 Phoenix brochure listed fourteen different models from a standard 100 at £119.19.11 through 150, 175, 200, 250 to the T325 with an electric start at £214.19.11. The brochure also shows the body with a cooling tunnel between the rider's legs suggesting the use of motorcycle engines to reduce costs instead of the fan cooled scooter units. Phoenix, one of the first British scooter manufacturers, made their last machine in late 1964.

Only five or so Phoenix scooters are known to exist, most – like the one in the collection – are the early 150s with metal bodies confirming the high number made in the early years of manufacture. The collection Phoenix is fully restored and won the 'Best Scooter' award at the Stafford Motorcycle Show in 2009 and the Bristol Motorcycle Show in 2011 – not bad for a scooter with a 'simple appearance'.

TECHNICAL DATA

YEAR	1957
ENGINE	147cc Villiers
GEARBOX	3 speed 2 pedal foot change
SUSPENSION	Front – leading link Rear – swinging fork
POWER	5.4 bhp @ 4,300 rpm
TOP SPEED	50 mph
COST (1957)	£147.4.0
CONDITION	Fully restored

WABO 1957

"The great bargain was the new Wabo scooter"

'SENSATIONAL OFFERS! The lowest priced scooter in the world' shouted the advertisement from Claude Rye the Scooter People. The scooter came with a 98cc and 147cc engine with savings of over £38 and £43 respectively. The great bargain was the new Wabo scooter – not a British machine but one made in Amsterdam – however, it did have a British Villiers engine. Wabo was short for Wagenbouw (meaning car building) a design specialist for the automotive industry, and the scooter was made by a company called Polynorm.

Two Wabo scooters were available a 98cc Villiers with a two speed change on the handlebars and lightweight front telescopic forks, and a 147cc Villiers with a three speed foot change and heavier front forks. The scooter had a duplex frame, no rear suspension and rode on 16" spoked wheels.

The rear body section was secured by four car bonnet type fasteners, the left hand door gave access to the petrol tap and carburettor, and the rear bodywork could easily be removed to expose engine, fuel tank and rear chain. The scooter had a very large engine cooling tunnel between the riders legs, a heel operated rear brake, two rubber saddles, a rear carrier and three attractive 'Wagenbouw WABO Holland' badges. From the front the scooter looked like a lightweight motorcycle with legshields.

How much did this machine cost advertised as 'the lowest priced scooter in the world' with savings of £38 and £43? The 98cc was quoted as having a 'today's value' of 125 guineas (£131.5s) and could be yours for just 89 guineas (£93.9s) – a saving of £38, and the 147cc (with heavier front forks of course) was given a 'today's value' of 150 guineas

(£157.10s) but was priced at only 109 guineas (£114.9s) - a saving of £43. Both came with a three months guarantee and a free 500 miles service. It looked 'a good ride to work machine' with full scooter protection and good motorcycle stability with its central engine position and large wheels. And what else could you buy for 89 guineas (£93.9s) – a 98cc Mercury Dolphin for £98-19-10 and the 98cc Excelsior Skutabyke for £94-17-3. A pin would be the only logical way to decide!

The Wabo certainly did not go down well in Holland – it is reported that in 1960 after the scooter had been on sale from 1954 to 1957 only 26 machines had been registered. Claude Rye only imported the machine in March and April 1957, again in small numbers – and it was still advertised in 1958 available with two-tone colours in Grey with Blue or Red for no extra cost.

Only three machines are known to survive in Holland and the same number in Britain – it was not exported to any other Country. A number of motorcycle companies in the Netherlands used Villiers engines, these were not made under licence but imported units, due to the small number of scooters produced no doubt the Wabo works had a good stock of 98 and 147cc Villiers engines for the rest of the country!

The Wabo in the collection – with a frame number of 0013 – has been restored as an apprentice project, the clips holding down the rear bodywork have been replaced by standard bolts. It is a tidy example of the very unpopular lowest priced scooter in the World.

TECHNICAL DATA

YEAR	1957
ENGINE	98cc Villiers
GEARBOX	2 speed hand change
SUSPENSION	Front – telescopic Rear – rigid
POWER	2.8 bhp @ 4,000 rpm
TOP SPEED	40 mph
COST (1957)	£93.9.0
CONDITION	Restored

BSA DANDY
1957-62

> "The BSA Dandy is – well just dandy!"

The BSA Dandy scooterette was shown at the 1955 London Earls Court Show. The BSA Group completed two prototypes a few weeks before the show – the Dandy and a large Beeza scooter with a 200cc four-stroke engine. Both had a good reception at the Show and the management instructed both models be rushed into production – unfortunately the Beeza never made it and the Dandy took over a year. The Dandy's aim, as a small 70cc two speed machine, was to gain part of the Continental moped market that was growing rapidly at the time.

It had a pressed steel frame with step through facilities with front and rear suspension running on 15" spoked wheels, legshields were standard but no footboards just motorcycle type footrests. The engine was a BSA design having a horizontal cylinder facing backwards, the whole engine and transmission was attached to the rear swinging arm suspension.

It was aimed at short home to work journeys and of course the housewife for shopping trips. The two speed pre-select gearbox was hand operated and it was claimed the scooter would give 135 miles to the gallon.

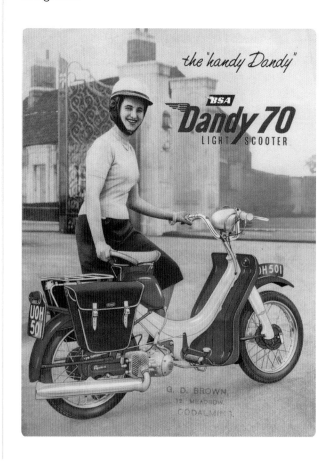

THE ALL-BRITISH LIGHT SCOOTER

Really dandy – anyone for tennis?

The Dandy in the collection has been restored in the original red and cream colours and has as extras a speedo (£2-17-7) and a tubular rear carrier with pannier bag supports (£1-13-10).

It was not long before BSA brochures were stating 'The BSA Dandy is – well just dandy!' and 'the handy Dandy' depicting gentlemen going to work and ladies off to play tennis on Dandys in Red and Cream and Blue and Cream. Most of the routine maintenance was plain and dandy except when the ignition points required adjustment – this unfortunately required the engine to be removed from the frame. One magazine reports that in 1958 (the height of the scooter boom) demand in the summer increased considerably and production had to be stepped up. The Dandy cruised on until production ceased at the end of 1962.

Interestingly the Dandy was not BSA's first scooter – one had been developed in the early 1940s and a number of prototypes were made, this machine was similar to those made in the USA at the time, however, unfortunately this went the same way as the Beeza.

TECHNICAL DATA

YEAR	1959
ENGINE	70cc
GEARBOX	2 speed pre-select hand change
SUSPENSION	Front – leading link Rear – swinging arm
TOP SPEED	30 mph
COST (1959)	£76.12.0
CONDITION	Restored

MOPEDS

Moving on from the cyclemotor phase most European Countries began making mopeds in high numbers from about 1953. The word moped came from Germany about this time linking the words 'motor' and 'pedal' for a two wheeler with an engine of up to 49cc that could be started or given assistance by using the pedals.

Although the term moped was in use in Britain by the mid 1950s the Power and Pedal magazine price list was still in the past and listed 'Motorised Cycles and Autocycles'. In February 1956 this list consisted of three Autocycles, five cyclemotors sold complete with a frame, and about twenty-five mopeds. At first glance five of these were from British makers, however, the Bown and Norman were German based machines leaving just the Mercury, Hercules and Phillips as 'All British Mopeds.' (Both Bown and Norman were small motorcycle companies producing other lightweight Villiers engined motorcycles at the time.) This meant the British moped market depended on three British bicycle manufacturers.

This statement was in reply to an entry in the 'Motor Cycle and Cycle Trader' magazine dated the 15th October 1955 which said 'I hope it will not be long before some of our factories announce new introductions. In case anybody has forgotten about it, there are still many customers eager to buy British.'

On the continent most motorcycle manufacturers had started producing mopeds; in Germany DKW, NSU, Victoria and Zundapp were making the 49cc machines, Bianchi, Ducati and Parilla in Italy, Motobecane, Peugeot and Terrot in France, Puch in Austria and the Jawa Motorcycle Company produced mopeds in Czechoslovakia. Some of the Continental Countries did have certain advantages – use of mopeds at the age of 14, relaxed registration/insurance laws, use of cycle paths and of course more sunshine. However it would be the early 1960s before the British Motorcycle Industry tried to catch up with a 'moped-like' machine.

All the features the public really wanted.

Many times the Power and Pedal Magazine asked the question where are the British mopeds? – their prayers were answered when another bicycle manufacturer brought the Raleigh moped to the market in 1958. On the Continent in 1958 mopeds had moved on a pace – an upmarket machine like the German Victoria Luxus 'with a specification which puts it in the Luxury moped class, yet at a price within the reach of every rider' was undoubtedly a beautiful machine. It had a pressed steel frame, swinging arm suspension front and rear and a 47cc Victoria engine with three speeds. So, was the new all British Raleigh moped built to compete in this market – no, it was built for the cheap end, or as the brochure put it the Raleigh moped has 'all the features that experience has shown are most wanted – simplicity, safety, sturdiness, reliability.' It was well made, but a little too simplistic – it had no suspension, no gears and not even a clutch. The engine was an old design based on the Mini-Motor cyclemotor designed by Piatti in the late 1940s and although this engine had the Sturmey Archer name it was in fact built by the BSA Group. The Raleigh moped was unfortunately like the dated British Autocycle in disguise.

All the features that are most wanted on a moped, said Raleigh.

By necessity Raleigh quickly revised the machine with a clutch and then introduced the RM2 with the clutch and a larger petrol tank, however, by the end of 1960 they began making the excellent French Mobylette range of mopeds under licence. As well as the number of British mopeds being few, a British moped engine was not available until July 1959. This Villiers two speed 49cc unit was used in some of the Norman and Phillips machines and very briefly in the Ambassador moped until 1962 when most of these companies came under the Raleigh banner and Raleigh's own range of Mobylette machines were the only ones to remain on the market.

The 'moped-like' machines produced by the BSA group were the BSA Beagle with a 75cc four-stroke engine and the Ariel Pixie with a similar 50cc unit, both machines were quite attractive but very late and only lasted the 1964/65 seasons. In the early 1960s the moped/lightweight motorcycle market was taken over by the Honda Super Cub and other similar Japanese step-through machines, some which are still being made today.

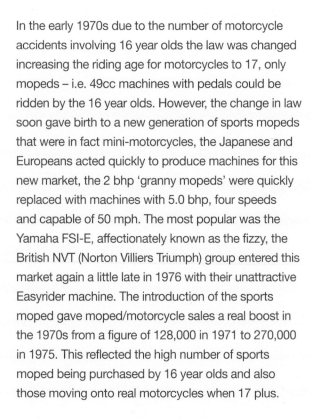

1975 Sports Moped – not for your grandma.

Mopeds with or without pedals are now restricted to 30 mph.

In the early 1970s due to the number of motorcycle accidents involving 16 year olds the law was changed increasing the riding age for motorcycles to 17, only mopeds – i.e. 49cc machines with pedals could be ridden by the 16 year olds. However, the change in law soon gave birth to a new generation of sports mopeds that were in fact mini-motorcycles, the Japanese and Europeans acted quickly to produce machines for this new market, the 2 bhp 'granny mopeds' were quickly replaced with machines with 5.0 bhp, four speeds and capable of 50 mph. The most popular was the Yamaha FS1-E, affectionately known as the fizzy, the British NVT (Norton Villiers Triumph) group entered this market again a little late in 1976 with their unattractive Easyrider machine. The introduction of the sports moped gave moped/motorcycle sales a real boost in the 1970s from a figure of 128,000 in 1971 to 270,000 in 1975. This reflected the high number of sports moped being purchased by 16 year olds and also those moving onto real motorcycles when 17 plus.

However, instead of reducing accident rates, unfortunately the sports mopeds brought an increase in accidents, therefore a further law change was introduced in 1977 to outlaw these machines and restrict the top speed of mopeds to 30 mph. The need for pedals was dropped at this time and the situation still holds today with the official moped classification full of restricted 30 mph scooter type machines.

DMW BAMBI
1957-1961

"Bambi is easily handled and very easy to drive"

DMW (Dawson's Motor Works) were producing parts for motorcycles including forks and wheel hubs during the late 1940s and started making their own motorcycles in 1950. The company made lightweight two-stroke machines mainly with Villiers engines for on and off road use.

scooter called the Dumbo, the machine had similar styling to the Bambi but was much larger having a Villiers 197cc fan cooled engine and an electric start with two 6v batteries positioned in a tunnel between the rider's feet.

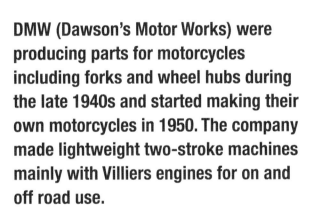

DMW Dumbo with a 197cc engine shown at the 1955 London Earls Court Show.

Their new Bambi scooter with a 98cc Villiers engine was shown at the 1955 London Earls Court Show but did not go into production until 1957. Along with the Bambi the company also had on show another

The scooter also had a long dual seat and a large rear carrier with shaped soft pannier bags, unfortunately this larger scooter never reached production.

Front of the DMW brochure, VMCC archives.

The scooter's body was designed with a rear carrier and this could be equipped for 'the occasional passenger'. In 1961 production of the Bambi ceased and the Deemster was introduced – a machine that was half scooter/half motorcycle and used the Villiers 250cc twin engine. It has been reported that approximately five hundred Bambis were made between 1957 and 1961 – most of these probably at the start of this period. With all the development work that went into producing an attractive monocoque pressed steel scooter the machine really deserved a 125cc engine. DMW ceased motorcycle production in 1967 but continued with engines and parts into the 1990s.

The Bambi in the collection is a 1959 model in fully restored condition.

The Bambi had a monocoque body with large 15" attractive disc wheels, the body pressings were produced by Elms Metals from inexpensive Kirksite dies made of a low melting point and reclaimable alloy, an ideal process for small batch production. The 98cc Villiers engine with cooling fan and two speed gearbox gave the Bambi a cruising speed of just 28-30 mph with a fuel consumption of up to 135mpg.

The lightweight Bambi had both front and rear suspension and was aimed at both sexes, the sales brochure stated 'Bambi is easily handled and very easy to drive' picturing ladies off to tennis, horse-riding and of course shopping. For the gentleman – 'Although small, Bambi provides a comfortable riding position for a 6ft. man.' – with the brochure showing a gentleman outside his bank with briefcase and trilby hat and another off to play golf with a full bag of clubs on his back!

TECHNICAL DATA

YEAR	1959
ENGINE	98cc Villiers
GEARBOX	2 speed hand change
SUSPENSION	Front – Earls type leading link Rear – swinging arm
POWER	2.8 bhp @ 4,000 rpm
TOP SPEED	35 mph
COST (1958)	£110.8.0
CONDITION	Fully restored

SUN GENI 1957-60

"Immaculate in design, modern in conception"

The Sun Cycle Company of Birmingham made their first motorcycle in 1911, after World War Two a 98cc Autocycle was produced from 1946 and a lightweight motorcycle from 1949.

Their first scooter – the Geni – was shown at the 1956 London Earls Court Show and production started in 1957. After much thought on scooter design the company produced a machine with a tubular frame housing a 98cc Villiers engine positioned well forward in a tunnel between the rider's legs. This configuration with 15" spoked wheels was chosen to give improved handling characteristics over the more conventional scooter with rear engine layout and small wheels. Although only 98cc the machine was a full size scooter,

however the dualseat was for occasional use only. Extras included a speedo, wire shopping basket at £1-15s-0d, rear carrier and a windscreen.

Guarantee No. 3505

PURCHASER

ADDRESS

MODEL 98 c.c. Geni Scooter COLOUR
FRAME No. YMS 295   ENGINE No. 410B/7084
DEALER J.T. Whittaker,
ADDRESS   218 Hornchurch Road, Romford, Essex.
DATE PURCHASED   REGISTRATION No.

ISSUED BY - THE SUN CYCLE & FITTINGS CO., LTD.
ASTON BROOK STREET, BIRMINGHAM, 6.

The six month Guarantee from Mr Whittaker of Romford.

The Geni brochure quoted 'Immaculate in Design, Modern in Conception.' Another brochure featured Marlene Sale on the Geni – Marlene was 16 and worked in the Sun office when asked to be photographed with the new scooter at Sutton Park, Birmingham. Her reward was to see her picture in the brochure and all the scooter magazines and of course a box of Cadbury's chocolates. Sun introduced their Geni MkII in July 1958 with improved footboards and stronger front fork construction together with a few other minor improvements.

Sun Geni with Marlene Sale from the company office improving the product.

The company was bought by Raleigh in that year and the Sun name only used on bicycles.

The Geni in the collection has never been on the road and still has its six month Guarantee card from the dealer J.T.Whittaker of 218 Hornchurch Road, Romford, Essex.

A more conventional scooter – the Wasp – was introduced in 1959 with a 175cc engine. Sun ceased motorcycle production in 1959 with the Geni going into 1960 and the Wasp until the end in 1961.

TECHNICAL DATA

YEAR	1958 MKI
ENGINE	98cc Villiers
GEARBOX	2 speed foot change
SUSPENSION	Front – bottom link Rear – swinging arm
POWER	2.8 bhp @ 4,000 rpm
TOP SPEED	37 mph
COST (1958)	£120.0.0
CONDITION	Original – unsold machine

DEFINITION OF A MOTOR SCOOTER

This book concentrates on British Motor scooters produced from 1946 – since that date a number of machines have been produced that demand an answer to the question 'what is a motor scooter?' Most riders would define a scooter by its good weather protection, enclosed engine, a flat platform for their feet and small wheels.

The conventional post-war scooter mainly satisfied these criteria however some scooterettes conformed to only a number of these design aspects. Normally these requirements don't bother the average rider but where competition is concerned there obviously has to be a strict definition set down by the governing body.

DMW Bambi scooter, wheels and open space within the definition.

So, the definition of a scooter was set down in 1960 by the F.I.M.(Federation Internationale Motocycliste) mainly because of the National scooter competitions that took place on the Isle of Man following the Island's Motorcycle TT week. The scooter definition states the maximum wheel size, the space required between the legshields and seat, the width of legshields and the size of the platform. The scooters with an engine cooling tunnel between the riders legs such as the Dayton Albatross and the German Zundapp Bella had sufficient space behind the legshields to conform with the definition, however, the 'scooters' that had their engine positioned behind the legshields like the Wabo, Deemster and German Maicomobil generally fell outside the definition.

Sun Geni, maximum wheel size within the definition but the small open space would require a request to the F.I.M.

The 98cc Sun Geni with large spoked wheels and a central engine position just meets the wheel size but just misses out on the space above the engine. In cases like this the F.M.N. (Federation Motocycliste Nationale – the Auto Cycle Union in Britain) could apply to the F.I.M. for a decision on a particular make and model and no doubt the Geni would have been classified as a scooter. However, companies such as Velocette with its 200cc LE (and later Vogue) and Ariel with its 250cc Leader could not be classified as scooters against this strict definition even though company advertisements did suggest the machines possessed similar advantages to the scooter with full weather protection on the Leader and footboards on the LE.

THE FULL F.I.M. DEFINITION OF A SCOOTER IS SET DOWN BELOW

A scooter is:

a) A two-wheeled motor vehicle upon which the driver can sit on a seat without being astride a frame and having a free and open space in front of the seat for the passage of his legs.

b) The minimum size of the space forward of the seat must be:
    i) 25 cm. along a line projected from the top of the seat and parallel with a line drawn through the centres of the two road wheels; measured from the front extremity of the seat towards the steering column.

  ii) Downwards at an angle of 90 degrees from that line for a distance of 25 cm. and measuring 10 cm. horizontally along the lower edge, thus forming a clear space of a minimum of 437 sq. cm. which must be clear of any obstruction of a permanent or of a temporary nature at all times.

c) The rim diameter of both wheels must not exceed 16 in.

d) It must have a kick starter or other starting device. The electrical and lighting equipment must conform to the International Convention for Road Vehicles.

e) It may have a body but if there are legshields in the form of an apron their width must not be less than 40 cm. The footrests must be of the platform type and not less than 30 cm. in length.

Notwithstanding anything in the above definition; where this would appear to include in the scooter class a machine that is plainly a motorcycle or where it would appear to include in the motorcycle class a machine that is plainly a scooter; the F.M.N. may apply to the F.I.M. for a decision as to the classification of that machine for sporting purposes

So, to define your machine all that's needed is a metric rule and A level maths!

Dayton Albatross scooter, even with the cooling tunnel the space is still within the definition.

with its engine position centrally does not have the open space required. However, no doubt making the necessary request to the F.I.M. would see the Sun Geni classified as a scooter.

DMW Deemster, no way big boy.

Still confused – shown are a few examples, take two 98cc British scooters firstly the DMW Bambi has the normal scooter type open area between legshields and seat and it also has wheels of 15" within the requirements. So it is a scooter by definition. As mentioned the Sun Geni still has wheels within the requirements at a maximum diameter of 16" but

Looking at two 250cc scooters the Dayton Albatross wheels are within requirements and even with the engine cooling tunnel between the riders legs it still has the open space required. Whereas the position of the DMW Deemster's engine and fuel tank completely excludes it as a scooter within the definition.

DUNKLEY S65 1958-59

"The Dunkley scooter is a winner for power, appearance and price"

The British company Dunkley produced prams from the 1870s, a gas car in 1900, motorcycles in 1915 and the pramotor (a pram driven by a 1hp or 2½ hp motor) in 1922. Based at Hounslow in Middlesex they started manufacturing two scooters in 1958, the 65cc S65 and the 50cc Popular.

For the S65, announced in February, they made their own 65cc four-stroke engine and used attractive bodywork from the Italian Casalini Company.

The whole of the body could be hinged forward.

"THE DUNKLEY SCOOTER IS A WINNER FOR POWER, APPEARANCE AND PRICE"

SAYS **JOHN SURTEES**

NEW 4-STROKE O.H.V. ENGINE FOR SUPER PERFORMANCE
"It's a real all-round winner!" That's the enthusiastic verdict of famous T.T. rider John Surtees after thoroughly testing the new Dunkley S.65 Scooter. He awarded the Dunkley top marks for performance, economy, appearance —everything. These All-Star Points show you why this brilliant rider thinks so highly of the Dunkley Scooter. Its O.H.V. 4-stroke 65 c.c. engine gives more power per c.c., no 'whiskered' plugs, easy starting and longer life.

Photograph by courtesy of The Motor Cycle.

★ 160 MILES PER GALLON
★ CRUISING SPEED 30 M.P.H.
★ CLIMBS HILLS WITH EASE.
★ CARRIES TWO COMFORTABLY
★ SWINGING ARM REAR SUSPENSION
★ ALL-IN-ONE LIFT-OFF BODY FOR EASY ACCESSIBILITY
★ CHOICE OF SMART TWO-COLOUR SCHEMES

£98·18·6
(INCLUDING £19·12·6 P. TAX)

THE DUNKLEY S.65
Miles ahead for all-round excellence!

78

Woof woof, nanny it's difficult to keep up with this new Pramotor.

As found in a nice shade of rust.

For engine maintenance the whole of the bodywork – including the legshields and footboards – could be hinged forward by undoing just two wing nuts at the rear located under the small dualseat. Dunkley was reported to employ 100 men who produced 90 machines a week many going for export, some of the factory facilities including the foundry were housed in World War Two Nissen huts. The S65's advertisement included the motorcycle racing champion John Surtees who said 'The Dunkley Scooter is a winner for power, appearance and price.' [John Surtees was motorcycle World Champion in 1956 on a MV Augusta and went on to be Formula One World Champion in 1964 with the Ferrari Team.]

The scooter was made for just two years in 1958/59, in early 1959 Dunkley was taken over by the holding company MG Holdings Ltd. who in May 1959 also took over the Dayton scooter company. Production of the Dunkley machines was moved to Daytons at Park Royal, London, but unfortunately by the year end the manufacturer of all Dunkley scooters had ceased.

TECHNICAL DATA

YEAR	1959
ENGINE	65cc four-stroke
GEARBOX	2 speed hand change
SUSPENSION	Front – leading link Rear – swinging arm
POWER	2.6 bhp @ 5,200 rpm
TOP SPEED	35 mph
COST (1958)	£98.18.6
CONDITION	Restored

DUNKLEY POPULAR
1958-59

"The only British scooter with a car type four-stroke O.H.V. engine"

In August 1958 just eight months after the Dunkley S65 became available the company announced their second scooter named the Popular. After the attractive Italian lines of the S65 this one was very plain – in fact it looked like something the scooter world had seen before, it had very similar lines to the Mercury Hermes of 1956.

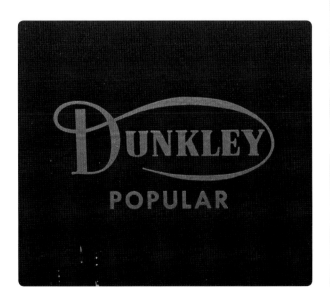

Dunkley and Mercury had been cooperating for sometime – the 1956 Mercury Mercette Moped had a Dunkley four-stroke engine and at the 1956 London Earls Court Show Mercury showed a Whippet 60cc lightweight machine that was in fact only sold as a Dunkley Whippet. So, to find the Dunkley Popular scooter having a very similar shape to the Mercury Hermes was no surprise – but it was confusing to the buying public at the time.

The Popular was another small long machine with telescopic front forks and a rigid rear end on 15" diameter spoked wheels. The engine was Dunkley's own four-stroke with a capacity of just 48cc with a two speed hand change gearbox. It was intended as a short distance utility machine that needed minimum maintenance and gave an attractive fuel consumption of around 130 mpg. Dunkley's advertisement claimed, 'The only British Scooter with a car type four-stroke O.H.V. engine is amazing value for money' and 'Brilliant road holding in all weather due to large wheels and scientific balance.'

In late 1958 after Dunkley had been taken over by M.G.Holdings they announced the Popular Major having an 'Engine one-third more powerful' by using the 65cc unit from the S65.

Obviously enjoying her choice of a Dunkley Popular.

Approximately 800 Populars were made and very few have survived – probably less than ten with just one Popular Major, the one in the collection has been fully restored but has a non-original saddle.

Just before the end Dunkley had a wide range of machines for a small company, their lightweight Whippet was given a box sidecar and named a Whippet Commercial, and with legshields it was called a scooterette. Furthermore, a very attractive motorcycle style Whippet Sport with the 65cc engine was also available.

The scooterette with legshields, dualseat, and powerful performance!

TECHNICAL DATA

YEAR	1958
ENGINE	48cc Dunkley four-stroke
GEARBOX	2 speed hand change
SUSPENSION	Front – telescopic Rear – rigid
POWER	2.2 bhp @ 5,200 rpm
TOP SPEED	34 mph
COST (1958)	£77.11.1
CONDITION	Restored

BOND PI-P4
1958-62

"The whole rear bodywork was made to hinge rearwards"

Having built 20,000 Bond Minicars over the last ten years Lt. Col. C.Gray – Managing Director of Sharp's Commercials Ltd. – stated in early 1958 that Bond have now entered the scooter market and created a 'quiet two-wheeled open car.' It was not the first time a two-wheeler had been called a car on two wheels and it was not the first time the Bond name had been used on a scooter.

Original shape of the Bond P1/P2 with a very large front mudguard.

After Lawrie Bond sold the manufacturing rights of his Minicar (Model A) to Sharp's he introduced the Bond Minibyke – half scooter/half motorcycle – to the public in 1950 and this was followed in 1952 by the BAC Gazelle. Again he sold the manufacturing rights for both machines to other companies – the Minibyke sold over 750 units but the Gazelle never really ran.

Another unsuccessful attempt was made by Lawrie Bond in 1956 with a prototype Sherpa scooter that never went into production.

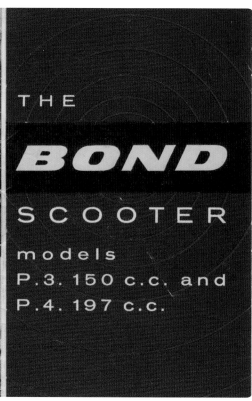

THE

BOND

SCOOTER

models
P.3. 150 c.c. and
P.4. 197 c.c.

So, it was no surprise in January 1958 when the Lt. Col. stated that having thoroughly tested every continental scooter of consequence Bond had made the new P1 scooter better in all aspects- this was a Sharp's designed scooter bearing the Bond name.

The company bought a disused mill and converted it to a factory, initially one scooter every 8 minutes would leave the gates and after six months the target was one every 4.5 minutes. The P1 (P for Preston) was a tubular frame machine using the new Villiers scooter engine with a cooling fan and a Siba Dynastart. It had a glass-fibre streamlined body with removable side panels and even a plastic petrol tank. If the scooter was indeed a 'two wheeled open car' it certainly came from the USA design school

having a two tone body with two large rear fins, chrome vents and alloy 'do-dahs'. It looked great.

A glass-fibre bodywork had been selected due to its successful use on the Minicars plus it did not rust, was easier to repair and reduced insurance premiums. It was also stated the front wheel and suspension was almost identical to the Minicar. The scooter had a roll-on stand aimed – as the Lt. Col. said – for the lady rider, however, perhaps the front moving mudguard with its massive front bumper was not to everyone's liking. Later in 1958 the P2 arrived with a larger 197cc engine and a four speed gearbox, cost of the scooters were £184.12.6 for the 150cc and £199.12.0 for the 200cc – both had electric starts.

In September 1959 production of the P3 (148cc) and P4 (197cc) were announced. The new models were given a front facelift with an improved smaller mudguard fixed to the legshields, the frame and engine were lowered for improved handling and the whole rear bodywork was made to hinge rearwards for easy engine access. It was a very nice looking scooter but still retained the American fins that housed reflectors or winkers as an extra.

The Bond scooters were a bold attempt to encourage people to 'Buy British' and compete head-on with every rival 'continental scooter of consequence.'

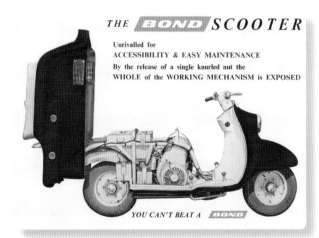

And rightly so, for with its non-rust attractive body and low maintenance cost Villiers engine it was a good addition to a short list of British scooters. Scooter production ceased in 1962 with approximately 900 P1/P2s and nearly 400 P3/P4s having been made.

The 1961 Bond P3 in the collection has been fully restored and has won a number of awards at past Bond Club Events.

Bond Minicars at the Amberley museum.

TECHNICAL DATA

YEAR	1961
ENGINE	148cc Villiers
GEARBOX	3 speed heel and toe change
SUSPENSION	Front – leading arm Rear – trailing arm
POWER	6.6 bhp @ 5,000 rpm
TOP SPEED	50 mph
COST (1961)	£178.10.6
CONDITION	Fully restored

MICROCARS AND THE MINI

From the mid 1950s a number of German Bubble Cars began to appear on British roads to join the Bond Minicar and the Reliant that had been available for a few years. In the November 1956 Scooter and Three Wheeler Magazine there was a full page advertisement and a two page review on the Heinkel Bubble Car, and news of a much improved Bond Minicar MK F that would be available in 1957.

The magazine also had a two page advertisement for an AC Petite, 'effortless and economic transport' for £392.3s.3d and a one page advert for a Powerdrive 'Elegance, luxury and economy' for £412.7s. The cheapest microcar was the Tourette from Progress Supreme – who built the British glass-fibre Villiers engine Progress scooter – at just £299. The cost of a powerful scooter like the Phoenix 325cc fitted with a Watsonian Bambini sidecar would have cost approximately the same money.

The November issue also reviewed the London Motorcycle Show that had on display the Messerschmitt, Gordon, Petite, Powerdrive, Reliant, Bond and Isetta. The most popular microcars at this time were the British Bond and Reliant and the German Heinkel, BMW Isetta and Messerschmitt. The Isetta was initially designed and made by the Italian Company Iso who made scooters and went on to manufacture Grand Touring cars, BMW made the car under licence and used their own motorcycle engine.

The scene: . . . Piccadilly Circus . . . The Lovely Pigalle Girls . . . and **Sabrina**, of course

Sole U.K. Concessionaires: **NOBLE MOTORS**

Unfortunately no room for another one!

The Heinkel and Bond are in the vehicle category known today as microcars, these vehicles in the 1950s were ideal for people who could not afford a conventional car or those progressing from two wheelers and motorcycles with sidecar who wanted to come in from the cold and rain (at the time it was easy to progress from a two wheeler to a three wheel car as the vehicle could be driven on a motorcycle licence).

The very fast 500cc four wheel Messerschmitt.

The 174cc Heinkel – that used the same four-stroke engine as the Tourist scooter – would later be made in Britain by Trojan with a 200cc engine, and the little Messerschmitt that began life as an Invalid Carriage would go on to have a 500cc engine, four wheels and a frightening top speed.

Invalid Carriage engines were also used for microcars and scooters.

The most exciting but disappointing microcar news in the November issue under the heading '80 mph – then you change into T-O-P!' was that the motorcycle company Vincent would not be producing a three wheeler. Initially this car with a 998cc engine at the back powering a single rear wheel used the 80 bhp Black Lightning engine with a top speed of 115 mph, but this left black tyre marks on the road and made the car somewhat unstable! Next the Rapide engine was tried with just 45 bhp but still returning a top speed of 95 mph, work on the car started in 1954 but changes in the hire purchase terms and a selling price of over £600 unfortunately meant only the prototype car was made.

However, all was well in the microcar business and more manufacturers joined the ranks, Scootacars Ltd made the only – rather tall and thin – British Bubble Car with a glass-fibre body and Villiers engine.

A British Scootacar MK 1 in red.

(Villiers engines were very suitable for microcars as since 1953 the engines had been available with fan cooling, electric start and reverse gears for the large Invalid Carriage market.) Another Villiers engine car was the truly beautiful Frisky with a body penned by Giovanni Michelotti; the Berkeley was a sporty number built by the caravan company using a design by Lawrie Bond, and the German Goggomobil was a miniature conventional car.

The sporting Berkeley designed by Lawrie Bond.

A miniature conventional car is just what Sir Leonard Lord, Chairman of BMC (British Motor Corporation) wanted. The Suez crisis and petrol rationing of 1957 made it imperative for BMC to have a small car with a good fuel consumption – but definitely not a microcar. Lord has been quoted as saying 'God damn these bloody awful bubble cars. We must drive them off the streets by designing a proper miniature car.' BMC's Chief Engineer Alec Issigonis was given the task having previously designed the popular small Morris Minor in 1948. He worked within the parameters of a 10 feet long, 4 feet wide and 4 feet high box. This he achieved by thinking outside the box with the engine in the front with the gearbox under, front wheel drive and small scooter size 10" wheels. The Mini was announced in August 1959 at a cost of just £497. At that time a Goggomobil 400cc was £486, a Frisky 250cc £499, the two German bubbles were just under £400 and the Bond 250cc cost £366. Not only did the Mini drive the bubble cars off the road it won the Monte Carlo Rally in 1964 with Paddy Hopkirk at the wheel and a 0 – 60mph time of 13 seconds – amazing.

Whereas the touring scooter with a sidecar had been surpassed by the microcar the cleverly designed Issigonis Mini now overtook the microcars. The 'bloody awful bubble cars' trundled on for a few more years and it was only the Reliant that was in a class above the bubbles that kept its following until 2002, giving the company fifty years of producing three wheel cars. The Mini was to have an even better history – however, with the increased size of the new Mini, the need for green transport and improved batteries for electric vehicles the microcar will return.

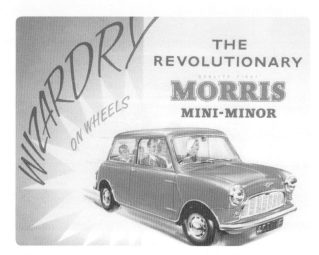

Brochure for 1959 Morris Mini Minor.

The attractive Frisky Sport penned by Michelotti.

This is my type of 3 wheeler!

PANTHER PRINCESS 1960-63

"Motorcycle testers praised the new scooter"

Phelon & Moore Ltd (Panther Motorcycles) famous for their 600 and 650cc motorcycles started to consider adding a scooter to their range in the mid 1950s. Initially they had a contract with the French Terrot Company to import their 125cc scooter but at the same time Panther had plans for their own scooter with a glass-fibre bodywork.

However, due to manufacturing problems with the glass-fibre they moved to discussions with Ernie Earles and his sheet metal company to use the Kirksite alloy steel pressings of the type that had previously been used for the DMW Bambi scooter in 1955. Dayton and Sun also had plans to produce scooters of a similar size so all three companies cooperated in the development.

Initially P&M imported the charming French Terrot scooter.

The Panther prototype with a front turning mudguard.

It took until 1958 before all three scooters were announced. The Panther Princess, Sun Wasp and

Dayton Flamenco all use a similar 2¼ inch diameter main frame with the same 175cc Villiers engine and very similar rear bodywork. However, all three companies showed their own individuality with the front of the scooter and detailed design.

Initially the Princess design had a front mudguard turning with the wheel but the production models came with a peak type mudguard fixed to the front legshields. The Villiers engine included a four speed gearbox and access was easy with just two hand screws to remove the side panels. The 10 inch diameter wheels included excellent 6 inch brakes and were fixed to the hubs on six studs. As extras a spare wheel and rear carrier were available fitting to three points on the main frame. A side hinged seat gave easy access to the petrol tap and carburettor and both electric and kick start models were made available. Motorcycle testers praised the new scooter and one stated 'the Panther Princess can be counted as an interesting and useful addition to the Villiers powered group of scooters.'

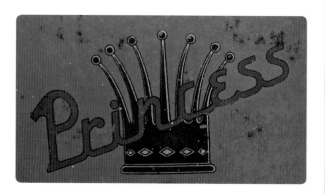

Unfortunately, following the initial work on a scooter in the mid 1950s Panther took until 1960 to get the scooter into full production. As the company missed the highest sales years of 1957/58 just 230 were sold, including three with a larger 197cc engine. The last Princess was made in 1963 and Panther ceased all motorcycle production in 1968. When the Princess was announced a Director of the company stated the scooter was the first stage of their plans to produce an 80 mph, 14 inch wheel scooter. At last British plans to rival the German Maicoletta – unfortunately it was just a British motorcycle industry dream.

Only about six Princess scooters have survived, the one in the collection is totally original and in fair condition.

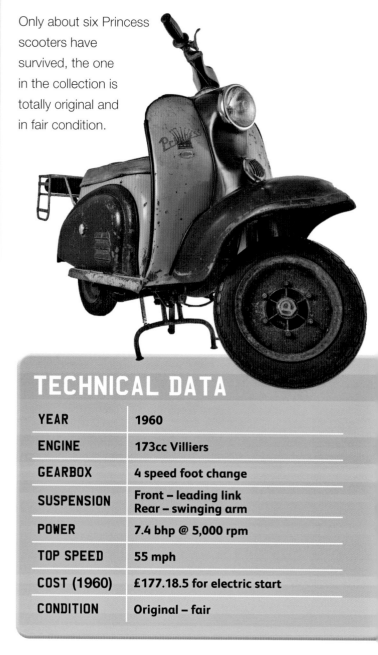

TECHNICAL DATA

YEAR	1960
ENGINE	173cc Villiers
GEARBOX	4 speed foot change
SUSPENSION	Front – leading link Rear – swinging arm
POWER	7.4 bhp @ 5,000 rpm
TOP SPEED	55 mph
COST (1960)	£177.18.5 for electric start
CONDITION	Original – fair

DAYTON FLAMENCO 1959-60

"The two side panels finished with rear lights"

The large Dayton Albatross scooter was specifically aimed at the top end of the market with the male scooterists and motorcyclists in mind. Obviously Dayton were missing out on a lower cost machine and one that could easily be managed by the lady rider. By joining Panther and Sun to develop such a machine would have been a welcomed opportunity and being one of the first British scooter manufacturers Dayton's experience would have been an asset.

PRIDE OF OWNERSHIP

The Flamenco had the smaller 175cc Villiers engine.

The new lighter scooter was called the Dayton Albatross Flamenco and seen for the first time at the 1958 London Earls Court show.

The front looked the same as the Albatross with curved legshields and a large headlamp, however, the platform was flat on the new scooter as the smaller 175cc Villiers engine included an integral cooling fan so the cooling tunnel between the riders feet on the large Albatross was not required.

The rear bodywork looked very similar to both the Sun and Panther except the two side panels finished with rear lights – a safety feature in case one side had a bulb failure.

The attractive and lighter Dayton Flamenco.

British Leadership - Superb Quality

PRETTY AS A PICTURE

From the sleek lines of the main body and side panels to the built-in " dual " rear lamp units, the " Flamenco " is not only pretty, but efficient as well.

Easily seen from this illustration are the large glove-compartment and lockable tool-box which are situated directly below the dashboard, incorporating an ammeter; the large expanse of foot platform gives ample foot room.

Road testers at the time praised the Flamenco's extremely pleasing appearance, its good road holding, excellent brakes and ease of using the wide centre stand. The last paragraph of the report said 'That we have found so few things to criticise on the Flamenco is a tribute to the thought put into the design. It should have a very bright future.' And so it should have had, alas, with the M.G.Holdings takeover in 1959 the attractive Flamenco had flown by 1960.

The blue and grey machine in the collection is in original condition with a low mileage and is still showing its large round Albatross Flamenco transfers on the front legshields and rear bodywork.

TECHNICAL DATA

YEAR	1960
ENGINE	173cc Villiers
GEARBOX	3 speed foot change
SUSPENSION	Front – swinging fork Rear – swinging fork
POWER	7.4 bhp @ 5,000 rpm
TOP SPEED	55 mph
COST (1959)	£189.10.0
CONDITION	Original – good

SUN WASP 1959-61

"Two toe pedals side by side making it easier for ladies"

As with the Dayton Albatross Flamenco and Panther Princess the Sun Wasp was announced at the London Earls Court Show in November 1958, a 150cc model was also shown but this never went into production.

The Wasp had the common 2¼ inch diameter Reynolds mainframe with the 175cc Villiers engine with a three speed gearbox – a four speed was available at extra cost. Like most scooters of the period it was directed at both the male and female rider, for the lady rider it had a low saddle height of 28 inches, narrowed footboards to assist those with

shorter legs and a two pedal gear change to prevent damaged shoes. Most two pedal changes were heel and toe but Sun went for two toe pedals side by side making it easier for ladies wearing dainty heeled shoes to make the change.

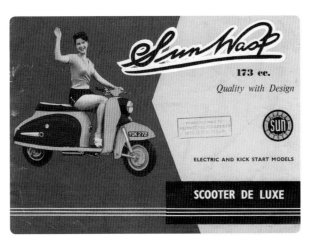

Two pedals side by side making it easier for white sandals!

In 1961 the Wasp Mk II became available with redesigned headlamp cowling, repositioning of the speedo for an improved view, a handle to assist with pulling the machine on and off the centre stand and a larger tool box.

SPECIAL FEATURES

1. Easily detachable side panels giving complete access to engine, rear suspension etc. The most accessible Scooter yet produced.
2. Full width glove and tool box fitted with detachable instrument panel.
3. Graceful lines and low seat height ensures easy handling.
4. Latex twin seat fitted as standard. Luggage carrier designed to accommodate spare wheel if required, may be purchased as an extra. Windscreen also available and other specially designed accessories will be available through our Service Department.
5. 'SUN' (patent applied for) 2-pedal forward gear control.
6. Aluminium Toe Plate Protectors.
7. Twin Heavy duty shock absorbers front and rear.

Also, a 6 volt kick-start model was introduced in addition to the original 12 volt electric start reducing the cost from £182 to £169.

Sun motorcycle production ceased in 1960 so the company could concentrate on scooter production – that was the good news, the bad news was in May 1961 a merger took place between Sun's parent company and Raleigh. By mid 1961 Raleigh decided to concentrate on their own Roma scooter and production of the Sun Wasp ceased.

The 1960 Wasp MkI in the collection has been fully restored with a few additional items like the coachlines and footboard edging strips added by the restorer Fred Day.

TECHNICAL DATA

YEAR	1960
ENGINE	173cc Villiers
GEARBOX	3 speed foot change
SUSPENSION	Front – leading link Rear – swinging arm
POWER	7.4 bhp @ 5,000 rpm
TOP SPEED	55 mph
COST (1959)	£182.14.11
CONDITION	Fully restored

VILLIERS ENGINES

In 1887 John Marston's Sunbeam Company started making top quality bicycles, however, he was unhappy with the quality of the pedals supplied by other manufacturers so another factory was established in Villiers Street, Wolverhampton – managed by his son Charles – to manufacture top quality pedals for their bicycles. Soon Sunbeam bicycles and all other quality bicycles were being supplied with pedals by the new Villiers Company. Villiers then began to make freewheels for bicycles and at this time Charles Marston bought the new company from his father.

One of the first 269cc Villiers two-stroke engines in a 1914 Coventry Challenge – BMCT picture.

[By 1901 the Sunbeam Company made their first motor car called a Sunbeam-Mabley described as a Victorian sofa with a wheel at each end and one at each side. In 1920 Sunbeam Cars amalgamated with an Anglo-French firm to form a new company called Sunbeam-Talbot-Darracq and in 1935 Sunbeam was bought by Roots Bros. In 1930 Sunbeam made a record breaking car called the Silver Bullet that was driven on Daytona Beach by Kaye Don who would start the Ambassador Motorcycle Company in the 1950s. Sunbeam also made motorcycles from 1912 until after World War Two when they produced their American style 500cc S7 and S8 motorcycles until 1958. Shortly after this the Sunbeam name was used on the BSA 175 and 250cc scooters.]

Following on from pedals and freewheels the Villiers Company made their first 350cc four-stroke motorcycle engine in 1912, this was not a great success. Mr Charles Marston was then reluctantly persuaded by a Mr Farrer to produce a two-stroke engine. Production of this two-stroke began in 1913 with a 269cc unit that was an immediate success. During the First World War Villiers did produce a few engines but most of their work involved the manufacturer of munitions. After the war Mr Farrer was appointed Managing Director and engine production commenced.

One of the many Agricultural machines using a Villiers engine.

Although initially designed for motorcycles the 269cc engine was used for a lawn mower in 1919 and this led to many other uses including outboard motors, Invalid Carriages and Industrial stationary engines. Although munitions work was undertaken again during the Second World War the company also made small four-stroke engines and the Excelsior two-stroke engine used in the paratrooper's Welbike.

When full engine production recommenced after the war demand was high for 98cc units for Autocycles and 122cc units upwards for motorcycles and Invalid Carriages. In October 1956 Villiers made their two millionth engine – this was fitted to a Francis-Barnett motorcycle and presented to the Science Museum. 1957 saw the company absorb the engine maker JAP (J.A.Prestwick) and at this time Villiers had subsidiaries in Australia, New Zealand and Germany with associated companies in Spain and India.

Immediately after the war the pre-war 122cc D9 with twin exhaust ports was used in the Swallow Gadabout MK I with a hand lever change, and the post war 122cc D10 with foot change used in the MK II Gadabout – no engine cooling fan was available at this time. However, by early 1950s variations were available as the engines were needed for Invalid Carriages, so options of fan cooling, three or four gears, and reverse gears could all be chosen. A fan cooled engine was used in 1953 in the prototype Oscar scooter. All 122cc engine production ceased in 1954 in favour of the uprated 148cc unit, this engine could also be ordered with a kick or electric start and with a cooling fan, the DKR Dove (kick) and Pegasus (electric) used these engines. In 1954 the Dayton Cycle Company wanted to produce a larger scooter and selected the 225cc 1H unit, however, this was not available with a fan so the scooter design incorporated a cooling tunnel between the rider's legs.

By 1955 the 197cc 9E engine was available with the fan and electric start options and this was used eventually in the DKR Defiant and Bond scooters. The 250cc twin 2T was made in 1956 with a four speed box – this was used in its motorcycle form without a fan in the Dayton Albatross twin and the DMW Deemster, later the DKR Manx used this unit with a fan and electric start. The largest 3T engine was developed in 1958 for microcars and motorcycles, and this 250cc unit bored out to make a 324cc engine was the largest engine choice for the Phoenix scooter.

Choose your British scooter but it must have a Villiers engine.

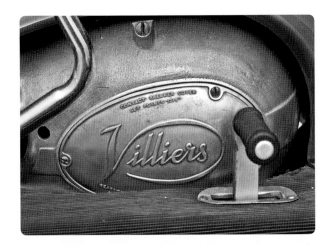

Dayton Albatross with Villiers 250cc twin engine.

At the end of 1958 there was a statement in the Scooter World Magazine about a Villiers Scooter headed 'No Villiers Scooter – Villiers stick to engines.' It went on to say 'Was a Villiers scooter planned? Rumour said yes. Rumour was so strong that Villiers have issued an official denial.' Mr. H. Geoffrey Jones, Villiers Joint Managing Director said 'It is not the policy of this company to build scooters in competition with manufacturers who are dependant on us for engines. Our interest lies primarily in the range of engines. These are incorporated in the majority of British scooters now in production and will be fitted to others shortly to be announced.'

Villiers celebrated their 60th anniversary at the Royal Horticultural Society's New Hall in London for three days from the 7th January 1959. The show was opened by Mr Farrer – by that time Villiers Chairman and Joint Managing Director – and Mr H.Geoffrey Jones. 275 British manufacturers using Villiers engines had display stands showing 100 applications including concrete mixers, potato cleaners, sheep sheering and milking machines. Villiers had 4,000 employees producing engines, freewheels/sprockets, non ferrous castings, steel drop forging, etc, at Wolverhampton plus other items at subsidiary factories including pressings, precision/special tools and even lead pencils under the name 'Master'. At that time seven British scooters were

using Villiers engines from 98cc to 324cc. The Phoenix with the 324cc engine and sidecar was shown for the first time at the 60th Anniversary Exhibition together with a DMW Bambi, Sun Wasp, Panther Princess, Bond and Dayton Flamenco.

However, after 60 glorious years the future was not good. In 1960 Villiers were taken over by Maganese Bronze Holdings who later took over the collapsed Associated Motor Cycles in 1966. The new company was called Norton Villiers – by the mid 1960s most of the motorcycle and scooter companies had ceased production and Villiers ceased engine manufacture. Spare parts and maintenance of the Invalid Carriages with Villiers engines was taken over by DMW and DMW's final Deemster scooters had to be modified to take the Velocette Viceroy engine in place of the Villiers 250cc twin.

Latest blower cooled 173 c.c. Mark 2L scooter engine

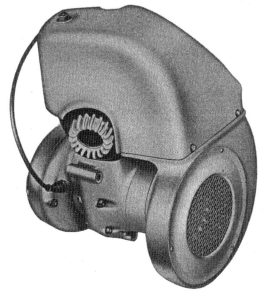

In 1972 the BSA-Triumph group were in financial problems and a new company Norton-Villiers-Triumph was formed with a Government bail-out, by now the end of the Villiers name was a few years away. Mr Farrer told John Marston in 1912 that he was confident he could sell thousands of his new two-stroke engines – he sold over three million and enabled Britain to have a scooter industry.

BSA SUNBEAM/TRIUMPH TIGRESS 58-65

"We can see a time when sales of scooters will equal sales of motorcycles"

Following the showing of the BSA Beeza in 1955 a decision was taken by the BSA Group not to proceed with production of the scooter – however, rumours about the Beeza's successor began to increase and multiply by 1957/8. In September 1958 BSA released advanced information on a new scooter which had been under development since early 1957. The machine would be sold under both the BSA and Triumph name [Triumph was taken over by the BSA Group in 1951] with both a 175cc two-stroke and a 250cc twin four-stroke engine. The scooters were shown at the 1958 London Earls Court Show and the full details of the three different machines were released at this time.

A new high standard in design is achieved by this brilliant B.S.A. Sunbeam Scooter, so graceful in appearance and so fascinating in performance.

The smooth silent flow of power, delightful ease of control, superb comfort of the suspension system, brilliant specification, economy and ease of maintenance are features which immediately identify it as the embodiment of Luxury on Two Wheels.

The new

BSA SUNBEAM

The machine's designer Edward Turner stated 'We feel the future of the scooter is assured. We can see the time when sales of scooters will equal sales of motorcycles.' If only BSA and the British Motorcycle

Industry had shared these thoughts in 1955. He also stated his five year plan included a scooter with fully automatic transmission.

The scooters produced under the BSA name would be know as BSA Sunbeams and the Triumph scooter as the Triumph Tigress – the three models were the 175cc and two 250cc twins, one having an electric start. Apart from the two different engines the rest of the machines were almost identical having a tubular duplex frame, a four speed gearbox, ten inch wheels and a fully enclosed chain.

The new scooter was certainly a good looker with a dualseat, a neutral selector, good road holding and due to its light weight was easy to manage and place on its centre stand. The rear bodywork included a small blister on either side giving access to the ignition points and adjustment for the clutch.

However, to take off the rear bodywork for maintenance about ten bolts had to be removed and if a carrier and spare wheel was fitted these also had to be removed. This was bad news – scooters had been available on the market from the Continent for five years where the whole rear bodywork could be removed (with carrier) by working on just one or two bolts. Furthermore, there was no storage space built into the scooter, no ignition key or seat lock, the covers over the batteries on the legshields were difficult to remove and the position of the exhaust pipes on the 250cc machine turned the rear bodywork into a radiator! So, some good news and some bad.

The original colours used were Sunbeam green for the BSA and the popular Triumph Shell Blue Sheen for the Tigress. By 1961 other colours were available including for the Tigress, Mimosa & Ivory and Grey & Ivory. Eventually the position of the silencer was modified for the 250cc which thankfully turned off the radiator.

"The machine would be sold under both the BSA and Triumph names"

In 1958 BSA was quoted as saying they were ready to produce 50,000 scooters each year, but in June 1960 they stated production had been upped to 400 a week, i.e. only 20,000 per year.

With their late entry to the market nowhere near the 50,000 figure was achieved. The 250cc twin production stopped in 1964 with the 175cc continuing until mid 1965. Meanwhile Mr Turner's five year plan for a fully automatic scooter was heading for fruition.

No ignition key or seat lock just a steering lock.

The 175cc Tigress in the collection has been recently fully restored, the 250cc twin kick-start Sunbeam is an older restoration.

The scooter had two access blisters, one either side.

Using the 250cc twin engine two microcars were developed – one an open top with motorcycle type handlebars and the second a saloon (which had a roof but no side-screens) using a half steering wheel. These were given the name Ladybird but were under powered, noisy and had indifferent handling at higher speeds so never saw production.

TECHNICAL DATA

	250cc	175cc
YEAR	1961	1959
ENGINE	249cc four stroke twin	172cc two stroke
GEARBOX	4 speed foot change	
SUSPENSION	Front – telescopic single leg Rear – swinging arm	
POWER	10 bhp @ 5,000 rpm	7.5 bhp @ 5,000 rpm
TOP SPEED	70 mph	55 mph
COST (1960)	£180.18.9	£159.10.7
CONDITION	Restored	Fully restored

EXCELSIOR MONARCH MKI 1959-60

"Enjoy the Monarch's zip was the slogan"

After testing the British scooter market with the imported Excelsior Heinkel and the Skutabyke the advertisements in the scooter magazines of May 1959 stated 'Excelsior great name in motor-cycling brings you the all British Monarch a great new scooter.'

It was certainly new for Excelsior but to the public it looked exactly the same as the DKR scooter. The Power and Pedal magazine stated 'Excelsior turn to scooters again', and 'most astonishing scooter news of the year is the recently announced 147cc Excelsior–engined Monarch scooter. To the eye the Monarch is a DKR machine from front to rear.' 'The makers of the Monarch frankly acknowledge the source of the presswork and other components but hold it is better to market the Monarch today than wait to the end of the year for a different design.' It therefore sounds that 1960 will be another year for astonishing scooter news.

'Enjoy the Monarch's Zip' was the slogan for their advertisements – the zip came from Excelsior's own 147cc two-stroke engine used in their Consort and Courier motorcycles giving 8.4 bhp against the 6.2 bhp from the Villiers engine in the DKR Dove. Unfortunately, this extra zip cost £6-0-0 over the Dove's price.

Enjoy Independent Travel with Your ---

Excelsior

Monarch SCOOTER

Issued 9-4-59

The Monarch came in two-tone colours with the makers engine and an Albion three-speed gearbox, two models were available the KS with a kick-start and EL with electric, the KS cost £163-15-0 and the EL £183-1-0. In 1960 the models were given new classifications, the KS became the MK1 and the EL was known as the ME1.

Excelsior acknowledge the source of the DKR presswork.

The Monarch brochure stated 'Advanced styling in design give the Excelsior scooter a most elegant appearance.' This advanced styling would only last a very short while as both Excelsior and DKR would be announcing even greater advanced styling for the 1960s. Excelsior said the development of a totally new scooter would cost anything up to £20,000 and take them nine months. Lets hope the new scooter has more appeal to the buying public because it was not long before large dealers were selling the Monarch DKR look-alike for knock down prices.

It is thought that less than five Excelsior Monarch MKIs have survived, the one in the collection has been beautifully restored in its original red and cream colours.

TECHNICAL DATA

YEAR	1959
ENGINE	147cc Excelsior two-stroke
GEARBOX	3 speed heel and toe change
SUSPENSION	Front – leading link Rear – swinging arm
POWER	8.4 bhp @ 5,000 rpm
TOP SPEED	55 mph
COST (1959)	£183.1.0 (electric start)
CONDITION	Fully restored

EXCELSIOR MONARCH MKII 1960-62

"The new scooter had a complete glass-fibre bodywork."

After twelve months of development and 'anything up to £20,000 costs' the new Excelsior scooter was announced in June 1960 for production on the 1st July. The scooter was called the Monarch MKII and as the Scooter and Three Wheeler magazine stated 'It's all by Excelsior this time' and 'Glass Fibre for a new British Scooter.' The frame consisted of a 2¼" single tube backbone with three channel cross members supporting the floor.

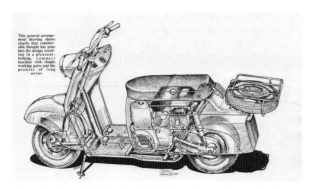

Drawing shows the Excelsior 147cc fan cooled engine and the two wing nuts under the seat to remove the rear glass-fibre bodywork. Mortons Archive.

The wheels were 10" diameter and quickly detachable – a well needed improvement over the rear wheel on the old Monarch. The engine was the same 147cc Excelsior unit with the Albion three speed gearbox operated by heel and toe pedals.

An Excelsior waiting to be a smart Monarch.

The new scooter had a complete glass-fibre bodywork consisting of six sections, the rear body as one unit, two sections for the footboards, two mouldings formed the front apron with a separate moulding for the front mudguard.

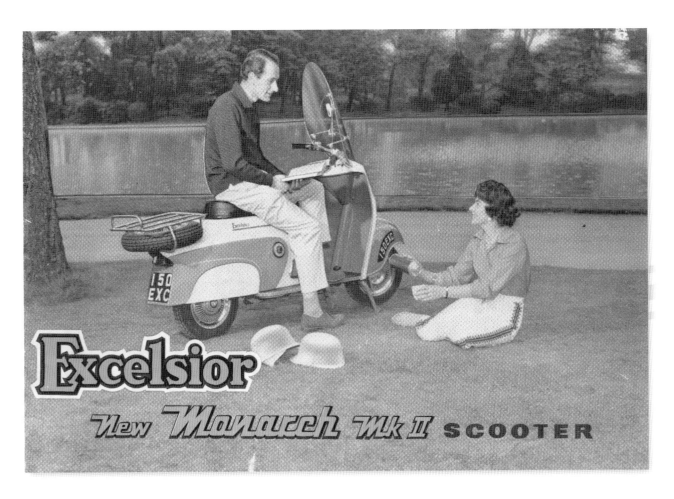

The rear of the scooter was a completely new attractive design, however, the front mudguard and legshields were a copy of the German Hercules scooter imported as the Kieft. The whole design was very attractive in two tone paint – also many extras were available including rear wheel side spats, wheel embellishers, windscreen, spare wheel and rear carrier.

Excelsior badges and a welcoming new seat.

The whole of the rear bodywork could be removed by undoing just two wing nuts under the dualseat which was kept in place with a snap fastener – what an improvement on the BSA Groups rear bodywork design. By October it was reported 'The ultra-modern Excelsior Monarch MKII is rolling off the production lines in quantity. For a start, the electric starter model is being concentrated upon.' The electric start machine (E11) cost £184 and the kick start version (K11) was £164. Both models were just £1 more expensive than the old Monarchs but due to the glass-fibre bodies they were forty pounds less in weight. Sadly the scooter lacked storage space behind the legshields and had very little security with no locks on the steering or dualseat. When the new DKR Capella scooter arrived later in 1960 it was evident the two companies had co-operated further with a very similar frame, front and rear suspension and the same method of adjusting the rear chain.

A British Excelsior looking very much like a German Hercules.

At the London Earls Court Show in 1960 a new Golden V model was announced with the Villiers 197cc engine, this new Monarch with its larger engine, wheel spats and embellishers, and two-tone paintwork must rate as one of the most attractive British scooters.

Unfortunately it was only in the price list at £195 for a short while and may never have moved to production. Manufacture of the two Monarch MKII models, known at the end as the K12 and E12, ceased in 1962 and all Excelsior motorcycle production ended in 1965.

Ready to go with a new Smiths 80 mph speedo!

Only a few Monarch MKIIs are known to survive with the best one in 'as new' condition in a motor scooter museum in Italy. Restoration of the one in the collection was finished at the end of 2011.

Glass fibre for new British scooter

TECHNICAL DATA

YEAR	1960
ENGINE	147cc Excelsior two-stroke
GEARBOX	3 speed heel and toe change
SUSPENSION	Front – leading link Rear – swinging arm
POWER	8.4 bhp @ 5,000 rpm
TOP SPEED	55 mph
COST (1960)	£164.10.0 (kick start) £184.10.0 (electric start)
CONDITION	Restored

TROJAN TROBIKE
1960-62

"One as a garden bike with no front brake or bulb horn."

Trojan Limited was registered in 1914 as a precision and general engineering company, they were immediately involved in the war effort but continued the development of a basic and inexpensive car using a two-stroke engine with chain drive and solid tyres. Trojan then moved to Croydon, Surrey in 1927 and began production of a commercial delivery van.

After the Second World War they produced a new 15 cwt van and in 1947 began the manufacture of the Piatti designed Mini-Motor cyclemotor with a 49cc two-stroke engine positioned above the rear bicycle wheel and driving the wheel with a roller on the tyre.

Trojan were the sole distributor for the American Clinton engine.

Trobike (A16)

The really featherweight runabout

Build it yourself for garden or road use

The engine was also used for lawn mowers, stationary engines and vacuum pumps for milking – also a 75cc engine was produced for commercial tricycles and other uses. It is stated between 1947 and 1956 some 70,000 units were made.

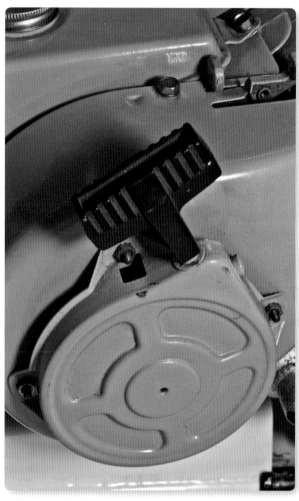

Starting was by a simple pull handle.

In the USA in the late 1950s karting had become a popular sport for those wanting the thrill of motor racing at minimum cost. The directors of Trojan had seen this new sport and by the end of 1959 had built the first British kart naming it the Trokart. Most of the karts in the USA had Clinton engines so Trojan decided to use these engines and became sole distributor. Karting in Britain took off in a big way starting with these Trojan karts, and now of course many Formula 1 champions have began their career on such machines.

Following on from the Trokart the company introduced their Trobike in early 1960 using again the 98cc Clinton Panther two-stroke engine. The tiny bike consisted of two hoop frames supporting the engine at the bottom and a single seat at the top with a top speed of 32 mph.

The Trobike can easily be lifted into a car boot or aircraft.

The machine had no suspension, plastic mudguards and chainguard, and just pegs for the rider's feet. Two models were available, one as a garden bike with no front brake or bulb horn and one for the road including a front brake, horn and of course a number plate. In 1961 a garden Trobike in kit form (no purchase tax) was just £35-10-6, a road bike was £39-19-6 as a kit and £49-19-6 fully assembled. This was scootering without frills and of course due to its size and light weight could easily be lifted into an aircraft, boat or car boot. It was not long before schoolboys were using the manageable Trobike to take their driving test, in fact part of the road test in the May 1961 Scooter and Three Wheeler magazine was undertaken by twelve year old Alice! This they said was 'A perfect demonstration that the Trobike is simplicity itself.' Starting was by a recoil hand pull, there were no gears and an automatic centrifugal clutch was fitted. Was the Trobike a good idea? – by 1962 the road model in kit form had been reduced to £25.

The bike was called the Chimp with advertisements stating 'Take a Chimp into the family – you'll wonder how you ever managed without him!' The writer of an article in the Motorcycle Sport magazine, August 1971, took it to the Isle of Man but with two up on the large dualseat it 'refused to climb even slight slopes', however, his children thoroughly enjoyed riding it in the fields. The price of a Chimp was £75 in kit form.

The 1962 Trobike in the collection has a white frame, a yellow Clinton engine and red plastic guards – these seem to be the most popular (maybe only) colour. The bike has been fully restored.

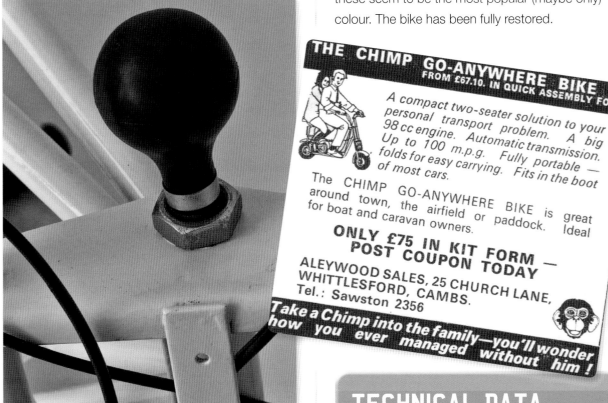

The road bike had a front brake and a horn!

However, a similar type of machine using the Clinton engine came to the market ten years later in 1969. It was announced in the Flight International magazine on the 30th October, 'as suitable for carriage in light aircraft as an aid to covering the last few miles of a journey.' The lightweight scooter was made by Aleywood Limited of Weymouth and again used a two hoop frame with tubing the company used for roll-over bars on racing cars.

TECHNICAL DATA

YEAR	1962
ENGINE	98cc Clinton two-stroke
GEARBOX	Single speed
SUSPENSION	Front – rigid Rear – rigid
POWER	2.5 bhp @ 3,800 rpm
TOP SPEED	32 mph
COST (1961)	£39.19.6 (kit form) £49.19.6 (fully assembled
CONDITION	Fully restored

JAMES
1960-65

"The tubular frame was positioned around the edge of the legshields."

Harry James formed the James Cycle Company in 1880 and the first motorcycles were made by the James Motorcycle Company of Birmingham in 1902. In the early 1950s James and Francis-Barnett joined AJS and Matchless in the AMC Group (Associates Motorcycles), both James and Francis-Barnett made lightweight motorcycles with Villiers engines.

In the 1950s a Director of AMC with his 'big bike' hat on is quoted to have said 'we shall never make scooters', however, a little later AMC started to make their own two-stroke engines (designed by Vincenti Piatti) with future plans for a scooter.

Definitely an advertisement for the scooter boys.

So the group did develop and build a scooter and it was sold under the James name and incorporated some novel and good design features along with some very tasteful advertisements.

The scooter came in two tone colours with the headlamp positioned high on the handlebars – however, especially from the front, the shape was an acquired taste. With the engine under the floorboards the centre of gravity and road holding were excellent plus it was one of the first scooters to have a large storage space under the dualseat.

The tubular frame was positioned around the edge of the legshields and down the sides of the machine so protecting the scooter and the rider in a spill. The engine used was the new AMC 150cc unit (also used in the James Cadet motorcycle) and was positioned under the floorboards with the cylinder horizontal and facing the front of the machine.

The front of the James was not beautiful but the scooter included some novel ideas.

A number of road testers said the handling, safety aspects and brakes were so good it could take a 250cc engine.

A lockable seat with storage space under.

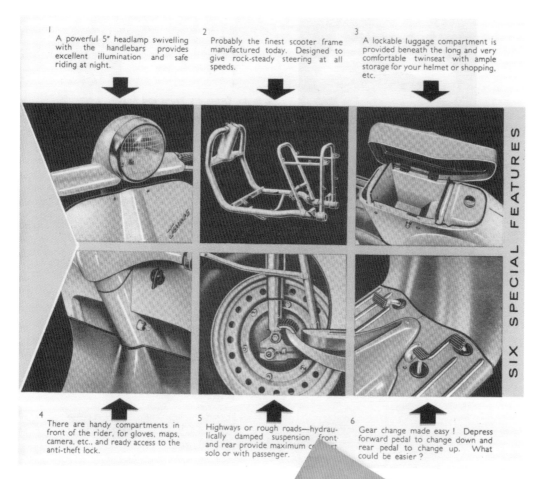

1. A powerful 5" headlamp swivelling with the handlebars provides excellent illumination and safe riding at night.

2. Probably the finest scooter frame manufactured today. Designed to give rock-steady steering at all speeds.

3. A lockable luggage compartment is provided beneath the long and very comfortable twinseat with ample storage for your helmet or shopping, etc.

4. There are handy compartments in front of the rider, for gloves, maps, camera, etc., and ready access to the anti-theft lock.

5. Highways or rough roads—hydraulically damped suspension front and rear provide maximum comfort solo or with passenger.

6. Gear change made easy ! Depress forward pedal to change down and rear pedal to change up. What could be easier ?

SIX SPECIAL FEATURES

In 1963 the scooter was uprated with a four speed gearbox but the engine remained the same. Sales of the James scooter were not good, the price which started at £165 had gradually reduced to £129-12-0 by September 1962.

Was the James scooter to be marketed in the USA as a Matchless?

The James in the collection is a 1961 SC1 model in very clean original condition with a dealers transfer on the legshields – W. Cusworth of Doncaster – and just 5,601 miles on the clock.

So, the new four speed model was great value for money but once again it was five years too late for the 50s scooter boom. Production ended in 1965 and AMC collapsed in 1966 bringing the end to both James and Francis-Barnett. The scooter had no name just James – at the launch the Press were informed 'You can have all your Princesses, your Queens, your Tigers, we're calling ours The James.' What a shame it had not been given the AMC 250cc engine and called The Matchless, in fact plans may have been made to sell the scooter in the USA using the Matchless name.

INSTRUCTION BOOK
150 SCOOTER
MATCHLESS MOTOR CYCLES
PLUMSTEAD ROAD, LONDON, S.E.18
ENGLAND

TECHNICAL DATA

YEAR	1961
ENGINE	149cc AMC two-stroke
GEARBOX	3 speed two pedal control
SUSPENSION	Front – leading link Rear – swinging fork
POWER	5.4 bhp
TOP SPEED	50 mph
COST (1961)	£165
CONDITION	Original – good

SCOOTER RALLIES

ISLE OF MAN MOTOR SCOOTER RALLY, 1962

JUNE 9th to 16th

The April 1958 copy of the Scooter & Three Wheeler magazine included an application form for the Isle of Man Scooter Rally - the write up on the rally with the form stated 'it's the sort of rally competitors like ... plenty of riding, solo events, team events. It doesn't cater for the spit-and-polish boys with Simoniz [polish] on the brain and a curvy girl-friend (non riding of course) on hand to enter in the "Miss ...." contest!'

SOUVENIR PROGRAMME — ISSUED FREE

The first Isle on Man Scooter Rally in 1957 was a three day event over the Whitsun weekend - it was a modest start with just 34 entries but it did include a reliability test around the TT circuit along with competitive events including a slow scooter race, team event, ladies race and ... Concourse d'Elegance (for the Simoniz boys), scooter girl competition (for the curvy girlfriend) and Loving Cup (best couple) contest!

John Glover on a Dayton Albatross at the 1958 Isle of Man Rally.

A Phoenix 150 at speed at the Isle of Man rally.

British scooters outside the appropriately named Villiers Hotel at the Isle of Man.

However, from the 1958 rally the format would change considerably – perhaps the magazine's comments on 'plenty of riding' and 'spit-and-polish boys' was a warning that in future the rally would sort the men from the boys and the women from the girls. There was to be a Monte Carlo rally type start from eight centres around the country with competitors travelling 250 miles with a number of check points to reach the port for the Isle of Man ferry.

Rallies and Shows can make you buy just one more!

A few riders made their way from Europe to the rally. The Rally was now one week long - followed the week of the motorcycle TT races - and included a 12 hour (one rider) and 24 hour (two rider) Regularity Test. For 1958 the entries rose from 34 to 191, these numbers would stay about this level for many years into the future. For the 12 hour and 24 hour test the scooters were divided into four classes. The 24 hour Class A, 200cc and above travelled 20 laps, 755 miles at an average speed of 31.4 mph; Class B, 151-200cc, 19 laps, 717 miles at 29.8mph; Class C, 100-150cc, 18 laps, 679 miles at 28.3mph; Class D under 100cc, 16 laps, 604 miles at 25.2mph. Any scooter with a sidecar was placed in one class below its engine capacity.

Each TT circuit lap is 37.75 miles and the climb up the Snaefell mountain road is 1,600 feet. The 24 hour test started at 12 noon and the 12 hour riders started at 9.00pm, so all riders drove during the night often in bad weather with rain and mist on the mountain roads and some with poor 6 volt lighting.

This was a severe test for rider and machine and proved the scooter was a two-wheeler that could do more than go to the shops or a day trip to the coast. Very few machines entered the 100cc class - in the late 1950s a 98cc DMW Bambi and a 74cc BSA Dandy did compete but had to retire, however, in the early 1960s the 78cc Raleigh Roma did well in this class. Unlike the TT races all the 12 and 24 hour tests were conducted on open roads, and all competitors had to obey the highway code while attempting to maintain their average speed.

Everyone is welcome on a scooter rally.

Most of the riders taking part belonged to a Scooter Club or a Manufacturer's Team. A machine analysis for the 1962 rally of a total of 174 scooters show Lambretta (50) and Vespa (79) being the most popular makes, scooters made in Britain included DKR (3), Raleigh (3), Velocette (1), Dayton (3), BSA (4), Triumph (1) and Phoenix (3). Obviously Lambretta and Vespa did well in their classes and the large German Maicoletta and British Dayton did well in Class A.

Phoenix had private entries and a Manufacturer's Team for a number of years with the company owner Ernie Barrett (ex TT rider) leading his team to success. In later years the 24 hour test was dropped and the 12 hour became known as the Manx 400 - the test was a little over 400 miles. The date was also changed giving a gap between the motorcycle TT races and the scooter rally.

As the British scooters had mainly Villiers engines the competitors stayed in the large Villiers Hotel on the sea front in Douglas. In 1960 Villiers engine scooters won 7 gold, 4 silver and 3 bronze awards in the 24 hour test. (Unfortunately this fine Hotel, one of the largest in Douglas - was closed down in the late 1980s and the site developed in 1997 with the Royal Bank of Scotland replacing the British scooter hotel.) Although the Isle of Man Scooter Rally was the major rally of the year the scooterist diary was full of other rallies.

Post war it was the Brockhouse Corgi that started the scooter rallies in 1948 with the Corgi club organising an 18-day camping rally in France, the club also started the first scooter races with a race for motorcycle journalists and TT winners being held at Silverstone in 1950. Following on from the Corgi success the first Vespa Clubs arranged a scooter rally in Bristol in the autumn of 1952 followed by the first International rally for Vespas at Brighton in June 1953. The first National Lambretta rally was held in May of 1955 and the 1956 rally attracted a total of 740 scooters.

VMSC rally in the sun at Lincolnshire 2010 including a red Velocette Viceroy.

Scooter rallies were here to stay with the first Isle of Man rally taking place the following year in 1957. Scooters were travelling long distances - in fact the Esso Scoot to Scotland involved a ride to Stirling, just west of Edinburgh, followed by a 170 mile endurance trail around the picturesque Scottish Highlands.

Belgium rally 2009 on a Triumph Tigress 250.

The first scooter race at Crystal Palace took place in 1960 – this was for production scooters of any capacity and consisted of 6 laps of the 1.139 mile circuit. Machines taking place included Heinkel, Maicoletta, Moto Rumi and the British Phoenix – the winning scooter a 277cc Maicoletta made an average speed of 54.29mph with a 174cc Heinkel taking second place with a speed of 51.30mph.

Scooter rallies and ride-outs still take place today with many Christmas Present or Easter Egg runs to children's hospitals, and many large rallies similar to the ones held on the Isle of Wight with riders enjoying the ride, their special type of live music and of course a few beverages. A weekend social rally has recently been introduced on the Isle of Man and in 2010 a Scottish scooter club arranged a Scoot to Scotland using a similar route to visit the past.

Isle of Man International Motor Scooter Rally
JUNE 25th — JULY 2nd 1960

Prize Distribution & Dance

FRIDAY, JULY 1st 1960
at 9 p.m.

at the
Douglas Holiday Camp

DKR CAPELLA 1960-66

"DKR had called in an engineer who was also an artist in styling"

DKR's completely new model was announced at the Normandie Hotel, London in October 1960 and was at the London Earls Court Show in November.

The shining new DKR scooter was made on the Pendeford Airport in Wolverhampton but it had something in common with a star 42.2 light years away, the new machine was named Capella after the brightest star always visible in British latitudes. Colour choices of Red, Lilac and Primrose Yellow with Old English White also made it the brightest star at the Show.

The new Capella was the brightest star.

Three models of the Capella were to go into production immediately, a standard 150 and 175cc together with a deluxe 175 having an electric start and a few more goodies.

The 150cc engine had a three speed gearbox and the two 175cc models included a four speed box. The old style 150cc models – the Dove and Pegasus were discontinued at this time. The shape of the old models had been criticised in the past, so for the design of the new scooter – which began in late 1959 – DKR had called in an industrial engineer who was also an artist in styling. His brief was to design a practical scooter that was good looking.

Both side panels could easily be removed and the seat had a strong hinge at the front to reach the petrol cap under the seat, however, the little flap to reach the plug made its removal very difficult. The rear wheel on the new model was on a stub axle

A full set of accessories for the lady.

and easy to remove and both 10" wheels were interchangeable with split rims. A novel device was also included to adjust the chain without getting dirty hands. The 175 de luxe was fitted with side alloy strips and three warning lights for ignition, low fuel and neutral.

Everyone at the show in November 1960 agreed it certainly was a good looker – very Continental like, the front and rear body was given a sharp line look instead of the usual rounded curves. The front mudguard, fixed to the legshields, had a flat top to take a small carrier and the headlamp and handlebars were given an attractive cowling.

Playing on the Capella name the advertisements stated 'This brilliant new star will draw the crowds', and there was more to come, in late 1961 the Capella 200 was announced – similar to the 175 de luxe with a chrome front carrier and heel guards as standard. The 200 had a similar top speed but speeds in the lower gears were improved along with its hill climbing capabilities. The brake horse power was increased from 7.4 at 5,000 rpm to 8.4 at 4,000 rpm. At this time the old 200cc Defiant model was also withdrawn.

The last Capella model announced in 1963 was a standard 200 without the electric start at a reduced cost of £164-11-0 compared with £173-13-10 for the de luxe.

As with the Excelsior Monarch MKII the DKR Capella was a very attractive scooter and both would have competed well against the Continental machines if they had been made around 1957/8. All five models managed to continue until 1966 when the star went out for DKR one of the last British scooter manufacturers.

The Capella in the collection is a 1961 150cc model fully restored in charming Primrose Yellow and Old English White. It has both front and rear chrome carriers.

TECHNICAL DATA

YEAR	1961
ENGINE	148cc Villiers
GEARBOX	3 speed heel and toe change
SUSPENSION	Front – leading forks Rear – swinging arm
POWER	6 bhp @ 4,500 rpm
TOP SPEED	55 mph
COST (1961)	£159.19.10
CONDITION	Fully restored

VELOCETTE VICEROY 1960-64

"Remember the days when scooters were just a giggle."

Veloce Limited produced motorcycles from 1904 and are famous for their single cylinder motorcycles and the LE (Little Engine) motorcycle used by the Police and affectionately known as the Noddy Bike. In 1955 the Works Director tested a prototype scooter based on the LE with a water cooled engine, however, this project was not developed further and by 1957 a completely new air cooled scooter engine had been finalised.

Unfortunately it took until the end of 1960 before the new scooter – called the Viceroy – was introduced. Engineering wise the machine was exciting with a 250cc horizontal twin engine incorporating a car type starter and driving a shaft to the clutch and gearbox near the rear wheel. The shape of the front of the scooter was not particularly attractive but very functional with the beak shaped front mudguard directing cooling air onto the two horizontal cylinders.

BUILT FOR MEN!!

A Viceroy—a man-size machine—costs under £200—about the same as an ordinary scooter.

If you never ride at over 30 mph, if you think of your scooter as just something to pop to the shops on, the VICEROY is not for you. But if you want a reserve of surging power, if you're looking for real roadholding and comfort, if you value high average speeds with perfect safety, if you're even vaguely thinking of touring Britain or the Continent . . . if you just want a better scooter, send the coupon below for news of the man-size VICEROY by Velocette.

VICEROY
BY VELOCETTE — MAKERS OF QUALITY-BUILT MACHINES

A very good period picture
of scooter and clothes
from the Viceroy brochure.

The gearbox was heel and toe operated and the
electric start lever positioned behind the legshields
so it could be operated by hand or a size 10 boot
– very masculine. In fact the advertisement slogan
was 'Built for men', other advertisements stated
'Remember the days when scooters were just a
giggle? The Viceroy is different. It's built for the man
who takes his riding seriously, who expects his
machine to take him anywhere.'

The instrument panel was a little dated.

Unfortunately, in 1961 the 'men' were spending
money on a new Austin Mini car not a luxury
scooter – so 1950s. With expectations to sell
thousands of Viceroys the company had only sold
690 when production ceased in 1964.

What to do with all those spare engines, DMW
used a few on their last Police Deemsters and a
new hovercraft company used three on each of
their HA5 Hoverhawks – two to drive the propellers
and one to drive a centrifugal fan for lift. Velocette
continued production of its LE and single cylinder

Fifty years of
the Viceroy
scooter 2010.

motorcycles until 1971, but having missed the
decade of the scooter in the 1950s they then had
to compete with the first decade of the Japanese
machinery in the 1960s.

The charming Viceroy in the collection is stated
to be one of two prepared in primrose yellow
for the 1962 London Earls Court show. Also, it
was awarded best machine at the Velocette LE
Club meeting in 2010 which celebrated the 50th
anniversary of the Viceroy scooter.

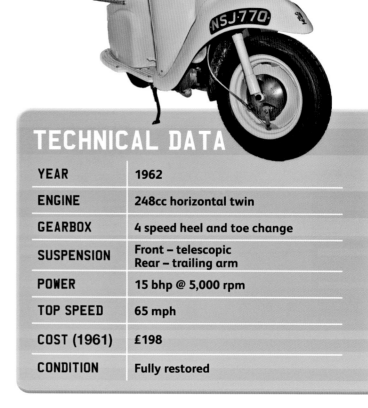

TECHNICAL DATA

YEAR	1962
ENGINE	248cc horizontal twin
GEARBOX	4 speed heel and toe change
SUSPENSION	Front – telescopic Rear – trailing arm
POWER	15 bhp @ 5,000 rpm
TOP SPEED	65 mph
COST (1961)	£198
CONDITION	Fully restored

AMBASSADOR SCOOTER 1960-62

"The sensational scooter – designed for economy and reliabilty"

Before the First World War Kaye Don took part in motorcycle racing, he then raced motor cars in the 1920/30s gaining many records including a lap record at Brooklands in June 1930 at 137.58 mph in a V12 Sunbeam. In the 1930s he also achieved a number of World Water Speed Records – one on Loch Lomond in 1932 at a speed of 119mph.

In 1946 he set up a company called US Concessionaires Ltd to import American cars and by 1947 made his first motorcycle with a 197cc Villiers engine. The company name was changed in 1951 to Ambassador Motorcycles based at Pontiac Works, Ascot, Berkshire.

The Ambassador had similar lines to the Zundapp Bella.

In the mid 1950s the Ambassador motorcycle range had increased to include 150, 225 and 250cc twin machines, and in February 1954 the works also began importing the German Zundapp Bella 150cc scooter and the 49cc Combinette moped. At the end of the 1950s Ambassador went with the flow and included some very attractive semi-enclosed motorcycles in their range including the Electra 75

Mr Franks on the new Ambassador scooter in 1960.

with an electric start. During 1960 the Chief Engineer Edgar Franks developed Ambassador's own scooter – six of these were shown to the public at the 1960 London Earls Court Show.

The new scooter, called the Ambassador, had a 175cc Villiers engine with Siba Dynastart and a four speed gearbox, the machine had front and rear swinging arm type suspension with 12" diameter alloy wheels. The side panel flashes on the scooter with the Ambassador 'A' were exactly the same as those used on the 1961 Sports Super S semi-enclosed motorcycle.

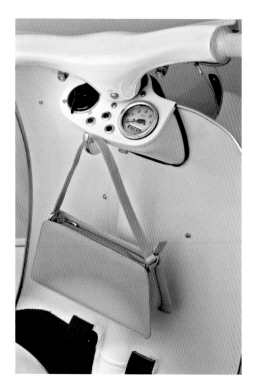

With a carnation pink handbag as a special extra!

Mr Franks stated the scooter had been designed with the ladies in mind being lightweight and having an electric start, low seat height, two pedal gear change, neutral and low fuel warning lights and attractive two-tone bodywork including grey and pink! It was no trade secret that the new scooter had a family resemblance to the imported Zundapp Bella, however, Ambassador were proud it was an Ascot conceived, designed and an Ascot built machine.

The scooter featured a fuel cap just behind the dualseat and just below the front of the seat was a small lockable compartment housing the petrol tap and glove compartment, both side panels could be quickly removed using the fast release Dzus fasteners to access the batteries and carburettor. The Ambassador advertisements and brochure stated 'the sensational scooter – designed for comfort, economy and reliability.' The company said they would produce thousands per annum – the scooter was in the price lists for 1961 and 1962 but only a few were made.

In October 1962 Kaye Don retired with the company having financial problems and Ambassador Motorcycles were sold to DMW, the Ambassador scooter was deleted by this time but a few modified Ambassador badged motorcycles were produced until 1964.

In the March of 1960 Edgar Franks with the help of Ambassador employees and motorcycle journalists had arranged a long distance destructive test on the scooter to eliminate all the problems prior to full production. However, only two scooters are known to exist today out of the small batch that were made – was this as a result of a mechanical problem escaping the destructive testing or the general decline of scooter sales and poor financial state of the company?

Side flash as used on the 1961 Ambassador Sports Super S semi-enclosed motorcycle.

The Ambassador in the collection was unearthed in February 2009 with just 3,850 miles on the clock and had been repainted in British Racing Green, the original colours were white and gold. It has now been fully restored in one of the other standard colours of the time, oyster grey and carnation pink, and was awarded 'Best Scooter' at the 2010 Bristol Motorcycle Show.

Gold and white Ambassador on the VMSC stand at the Stafford Classic Bike Show 2010.

TECHNICAL DATA

YEAR	1961
ENGINE	173cc Villiers
GEARBOX	4 speed heel and toe change
SUSPENSION	Front – leading link Rear – swinging fork
POWER	7 bhp @ 5,000 rpm
TOP SPEED	55 mph
COST (1961)	£180.0.8
CONDITION	Fully restored

DMW DEEMSTER 1961-66

"Twin wind-tone horns and a mercurial brake light switch."

The DMW Deemster of 1961 combined scooter weather protection with the weight distribution and handling of a motorcycle. The machine was designed by DMW's engineer Mike Riley housing the Villiers 250cc twin engine positioned between the rider's legs with a large metal box section above supporting the tank and dualseat with storage space under.

In profile the Deemster takes on a definite motorcycle appearance.

Further unusual features included twin front headlamps that could be adjusted from the handlebars, twin wind-tone horns and a mercurial brake light switch which operated when the front or rear brake was applied.

The machine also used bodywork items from past scooters – a front mudguard and legshields similar to those used on the Dayton Albatross Continental and side panels similar to the Dayton Flamenco. The Villiers 250cc engine could be ordered with a kick or electric start. A prototype Deemster was also developed with a BSA Sunbeam/Triumph Tigress 250cc engine with a shaft drive, this never went into production.

Obviously pleased with her twin headlamps and wind-tone horn.

A motorcycle tester at the time stated its performance and handling was way above the average scooter and its comfort and weather protection above the average motorcycle.

DMW modified the civilian Deemster for police use adding a large front fairing and a radio telephone positioned at the rear with the hand set on the tank. Obviously the large box under the seat plus the two large cubby holes behind the legshields were a further advantage for storing the many items of police equipment.

Police machines were the majority of the Deemster production and were available in black or white. When the Villiers 250 twin engine was no longer available the final 40 or so Police Deemsters were built with the Velocette Viceroy 250cc horizontal twin engine and shaft drive. The front mudguard was changed to a similar style to the Viceroy directing cooling air onto the engine. The last Deemsters were produced in 1966 and the company ceased all motorcycle production the following year.

Many more of the police Deemsters were made and have survived compared with the civilian style machine in the collection – this example was originally supplied by the motorcycle dealer Meeton and Ward of Surrey.

Police Deemster showing large fairing and radio telephone.

TECHNICAL DATA

YEAR	1961
ENGINE	249cc Villiers twin
GEARBOX	4 speed foot change
SUSPENSION	Front – leading link forks Rear – swinging fork
POWER	15 bhp @ 5,500 rpm
TOP SPEED	68 mph
COST (1961)	£232
CONDITION	Restored

RALEIGH ROMA 1960-64

> "You quickly realise that the Roma is a very fine machine indeed."

The Raleigh Roma scooter was an Italian Bianchi Orsetta (little bear) made under licence by the bicycle company Raleigh of Nottingham who had been making mopeds since 1958. Production of the Roma commenced in 1960 – it was an attractive lightweight scooter with a 78cc two-stroke engine and three speed hand change.

The horizontal engine hung from a large diameter frame which was cooled by passing air from a large scoop on top of the front mudguard. The set up was very similar to the earlier designed Piatti scooter.

Access to the engine was novel, using plastic finger nuts both sides of the engine cover hinged down to expose the carburettor and cable adjusters as well as forming a shelf for tools. Removal of the top cover was also easy giving complete access to the engine.

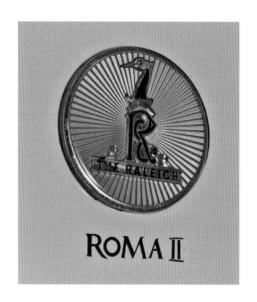

ROMA II

RALEIGH ROMA SCOOTER

The engine cover hinges down to form a shelf for tools.

The Roma was a powerful little machine for its size and won a number of awards in 1962 at the Isle of Man Scooter Rally.

The Scooter World magazine was proud to mention this and stated 'You quickly realise that the Roma is a very fine machine indeed, one that will stand up to all the hard work you can give it, while yet remaining docile in traffic and a pleasure to the eye.' The cost of the Roma in 1960 was £115.10.0.

From October 1962 the Roma II was available, it had a new plastic headlamp cowling, new exhaust system and increase power from 3.7 to 4.3 bhp. This did not increase the top speed but gave more power in the lower gears – ideal for two-up travel in town centres. Mid 1964 saw the Roma III with a few detail changes including a light alloy cylinder barrel – unfortunately sales of the Bianchi Orsetta were falling off in Italy and by the end of 1964 Raleigh had to end production of the Roma.

The Roma was shown with Cliff Richard in a scooter magazine with the caption 'The new lightweight scooter Roma, seen here with a pop singer called Cliff Richard.' This was in 1960 before the Roma and the 'pop singer' were famous!

A pop singer called Cliff Richard.

The Roma in the collection is a 1962 Roma II that has been fully restored showing the pleasure to the eye of this lightweight scooter.

Another Roma model – Cliff would not be impressed!

RALEIGH ROMA

THE LATEST AND MOST EXCITING SCOOTER WITH ITALIAN STYLING

TECHNICAL DATA

YEAR	1962
ENGINE	78cc
GEARBOX	3 speed handlebar control
SUSPENSION	Front – trailing links Rear – trailing forks
POWER	4.3 bhp @ 6,500 rpm
TOP SPEED	43 mph
COST (1960)	£115.10.10
CONDITION	Fully restored

SCOOTER ACCESSORIES

Mod revival scooters with accessory overload, Brighton 2011.

In the 1957 Scooter Year Book there was an article on scooter accessories by C.E.Allen that stated in large print "For every £1 spent on scooters, you can estimate that 2s (i.e. 10% more) will be spent on ... accessories."

It was estimated that half of that 10% was spent on functional items and half on comfort and enhancements for the machine.

The most popular functional items were windscreens and items to carry luggage. Unlike the average motorcyclist the scooter riders preferred a windscreen to protect their body and clothes from

C. E. Allen discusses the boom in scooter accessories . . . . . some functional, others serving merely to gild the lily . . . which represents big business to manufacturers these days

the rain and wind – in the late 1950s it was estimated that four out of five scooters were fitted with windscreens.

Very few scooters had a windscreen included in their original design apart from the German Maicomobil and the British Harper, most needed a screen clamped to the handlebars and used differing methods in an attempt to stop the rain and cold passing through the gap between the windscreen blade and the top of the legshields.

Camp with NANNUCCI

Two fine carriers are illustrated here—one for each end of the scooter. There are many others.

RIGHT: Rear folding chrome carrier, fitted with springs. No drilling required. Exceptional finish. Has provision for spare wheel. Supplied complete with two supporting stays. Single bolt fitting underneath dual saddle. Suitable for Vespa £4-15-0 125/59, 150/59.

LEFT: Front carrier suitable for all Vespa models. No drilling required. Heavy chrome finish. Fitted with internal spring and thick rubber bushes to prevent damage to body. £3-17-6

Apply to your local dealer or direct to Nannucci Ltd for illustrated list and name and address of your nearest stockist.

Nannucci Ltd.

5-6 NEWMAN PASSAGE
LONDON, W.1
Tel: Mus. 8112

The James ISO SCOOTER

PRICE INCLUDING PURCHASE TAX
£150-6-0

BRUCE LEWIN LTD
The Motor Cycle & Scooter People
17 NARBOROUGH ROAD
LEICESTER TELEPHONE
58580

ACCESSORIES

Triple Suite Complete comprising :		Front Fixing Scooter Bag	£7 12 6
Suit Case and Two Panniers	£7 3 1	Rear View Mirror (Screen fixing)	16 6
Two Pannier Brackets	17 0	Rim Embellishers (Set of 4)	£3 12 6
Windscreen	£5 19 6	Rear Carrier	£2 12 6
		Spare Wheel Assembly	£5 4 6

JAMES MOTOR CYCLES LTD · GREET · BIRMINGHAM 11
Telephone : VICTORIA 2211 (5 lines) · Telegram : JAMESGREET, BIRMINGHAM (TELEX)

More weight on the back and that's before the clothes are packed.

The most popular way of carrying luggage on a scooter was the rear carrier – this did nothing to help the weight distribution of the machine which was already light at the front end. Aware of this situation some manufacturers did in fact fit front carriers including the Piatti and Heinkel and some located the petrol tank in the front like the CZ Cezeta, Hercules and the DKR Dove. Some rear carriers also provided for two side pannier bags which made the situation even worse. For small amounts of luggage a metal or cloth (normally in the tartan style) bag could be fitted behind the scooter legshields. In the early 1960s the glass-fibre Skootokaddy was made to fit over the front mudguard of some Italian scooters, this large glass-fibre box, along with panniers and a rear carrier box, were made by Max Rhiando son of 'Spike' Rhiando who designed the glass-fibre Harper scooter.

protection, luggage facilities and improved comfort on the scooter the enhancements and chrome doo-dahs were endless. Front and rear bumpers, side panel strips, decorative port holes, toe protectors and wheel trims could all be had along with flag masts and even radios. In the late 1950s and early 1960s one or two mirrors were fitted for improved rear vision and a spot or fog lamp as a practical addition to the machine's headlamp.

However, a few years later as part of the Mod Culture it was not unusual to see twenty mirrors and twenty extra lamps fitted to the front of a treasured Vespa or Lambretta – at least it assisted with the weight distribution!

INVEST IN THE BEST
BUY "FULLY GUARANTEED"
RHIANDO
"RHITEGLASS"
EQUIPMENT

" SCOOTOKADDY "
RETAIL PRICE £9. 19. 6.
(illustrated)
DE LUXE £12. 0. 0. (with locks)
● LOCK EXTRA - 2 KEYS 17/6
● MATCHING COLOURS
● SPACIOUS CONTAINERS
FOR ALL
LAMBRETTA · VESPA · ISO
AND OTHER MODELS
SEE YOUR DEALER OR WRITE FOR BROCHURE
RHIANDO PRODUCTS
219 STOUGHTON ROAD · GUILDFORD · SURREY
REGD. DESIGN AND PATENT APPLIED FOR.

" HANDYKADDY "
RETAIL PRICE £3. 19. 6. each

" KADDYETTES "
RETAIL PRICE £3. 12. 6. (illustrated)
£2. 19. 6.

The comfort and enhancement type of accessory included replacing the original saddle seats with a more attractive dualseat, fitting improved footrests for the pillion rider and fitting rubber mats to protect the footboards. Once the rider had provided weather

Attractive accessories on a Lambretta at a rally in Belgium 2011.

TRIUMPH TINA 1962-65

"The little Tina with a dualseat was charming to see."

One year after stating his five year plan included a scooter with fully automatic transmission Edward Turner filed a patent for such a machine in May 1959.

'Fairy' was the first name given to this new scooter – thankfully this was changed at the last moment and the Triumph Tina was proudly launched at the Festival Halls in London in March 1962 – it was said to have caused a sensation.

The automatic transmission was by vee-belt.

"No gears, no clutch, goes at a touch" stated the advertisements for Turner's new baby.

The little 100cc two-stroke forward facing horizontal fan cooled engine drove the 8" rear wheel by a belt and helical gears. The automatic transmission was by vee-belt on pulleys which were controlled by a centrifugal governor providing infinite variable gear ratios. Fitted behind the headlamp was a start/drive switch operating an electrical cut-out to prevent the scooter moving forward accidentally, particularly when starting.

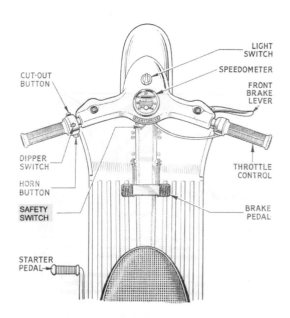

WORLD'S FIRST FULLY AUTOMATIC SCOOTER AT LESS THAN £100!

Oh dear – behind the scenes the BSA Group had launched the Fairy/Tina with virtually no prototype testing, the Experimental Department could not get a machine for thorough testing, and the Group – at great expense – had built a new building capable of producing well in excess of 1,000 Tinas each week.

The little lilac Tina with a dualseat was charming to see, the nearside rear panel was removable for access to the carburettor and the new automatic transmission. Unfortunately, the scooter had no storage facilities but a number of extras were available including a legshield bag, pannier bags, a windscreen and mirrors. The June 1962 copy of the Power and Pedal magazine certainly liked the scooter stating 'Tina is a delightful and efficient machine with very little to go wrong.'

Showing the safety start/drive switch, take control or it will think for itself.

A pretty Tina with extra stripes.

At a Press release photo shoot Edward Turner thought the switch was in 'start' and revved the engine in the 'drive' position – obviously the scooter shot off and it then hit a kerb and Turner took a tumble. Now it was back to the drawing board – sometimes you don't want 'a scooter that thinks for itself!'

The delightful Tina in the collection is fully restored with 6,731 miles on the clock.

Before back to the drawing board it was back to the Triumph dealer with many things that had gone wrong, frames bending, engines impossible to start and automatic transmission jamming solid. Unfortunately a lot of these customers were ladies that the advertising promotion had focused on.

Also, there was trouble with that start/drive switch and the advertising slogan 'a scooter that thinks for itself!'

TECHNICAL DATA

YEAR	**1964**
ENGINE	**100cc Triumph two-stroke**
GEARBOX	**Automatic transmission by belt**
SUSPENSION	**Front – single trailing arm** **Rear – swinging arm**
POWER	**4.5 bhp @ 5,000 rpm**
TOP SPEED	**45 mph**
COST (1962)	**£91.17.5**
CONDITION	**Restored**

TRIUMPH T10
1965-70

"By 1965 the old Tina had become the new Triumph T10."

Bert Hopwood was the man in charge of sorting out the many design problems with the Tina. He states in his book 'Whatever happened to the British Motorcycle Industry' that the Tina gave him a major thankless task which involved redesigning nearly every component of the scooter.

By 1965 the old Tina became the new Triumph T10, as well as correcting the design faults the scooter now had a more balanced and slightly larger rear bodywork – the overall length had increased by five inches and a larger dualseat was fitted. The engine was the same 100cc unit and the same size wheels and brakes were used. The T10 was given a few cosmetic improvements with a chrome top to the headlamp, chrome legshield edging and a side grill. Triumph still tried to sell it as a family second vehicle

'There is a place in every household for the Triumph Automatic and not many days in the year when she would not be used by one or other of the family.'

Edward Turner's start/drive switch had also gone automatic – this was now a pressure switch positioned under the seat, it was in the start position with no-one on the seat and changed to the drive position as the rider sat down. However, at the T10 launch the Press were informed when the rider sits on the seat the scooter can be ridden away – oh dear, the switch was set for a 10 stone rider and the slim attractive lady just sat there with the engine revving as she only weighed 8 stone!

The T10 was designed as a family machine.

[The new British Triumph Motorcycle company at Hinckley in Leicestershire produced 49,000 bikes in 2010 and exported them to 31 Countries – the proud Triumph name has clearly pulled itself far away from naughty Tina.]

The attractive T10 in the collection is in totally original condition with just 180 miles on the clock. It looks delightful in Mimosa and Ivory.

Perhaps as sales were not as great as expected Triumph experimented with three and four wheel Tina/T10 derivatives. Using a flexible joint on the three wheeler truck the rider was able to lean as with a normal two-wheeler, the machine also had a small loading area behind the rider's seat; only about ten of these were made and a few survive in collections today. The four wheeler was two scooters bolted together with a large seat for two sitting side by side and thankfully just one set of handlebar controls. Only one prototype was made and spent its working life around the factory nicknamed 'double trouble'.

Edward Turner had the right vision with his automatic transmission – what a shame this first early British machine had so many problems. The modern automatic scooter called 'twist and go' machines have eliminated the start/drive switch and can only be started with a brake being applied – now the world is full of them with engine sizes up to 850cc for scooters and a few motorcycles with even larger engine sizes. The automatic transmission plan was correct but its implementation too problematic, another missed opportunity for the British scooter industry.

TECHNICAL DATA

YEAR	1967
ENGINE	100cc Triumph two-stroke
GEARBOX	Automatic transmission by belt
SUSPENSION	Front – single trailing arm Rear – swinging arm
POWER	4.5 bhp @ 5,000 rpm
TOP SPEED	45 mph
COST (1965)	£109.4.0
CONDITION	Original – excellent

WINN CITY BIKE 1966-68

"This consisted of a monocoque glass-fibre body housing a 12 volt battery."

It was a good plan – drive to the outskirts of the City or Town in a quiet pollution free car, park the car, remove from the boot the small quiet and pollution free bike and ride to the office.

Members of the Winn family are building a collection, Amberley 2008.

It would be a good plan in 2012 but this was Mr Winn's plan in the early 1960s. Russell Winn was an electrical engineer who left Mullard Research and set up his own company Telearchives Ltd of Brighton to pursue such projects. By the mid 1960s he had moved to Oxfordshire and built the first Winn City Car having two seats, and three wheels steering from the front single wheel.

The car was of course battery powered with a novel design, the whole front of the body lifted up under its own power and came to rest behind the driver giving easy access to the seats.

The steering column could also be moved to the side making entrance to the vehicle that much easier.

The Winn City Car was not progressed due to the normal problems of battery capacity and vehicle range, but the Winn City Bike was moved to the production phase. A new company – High Speed Motors Ltd of Witney, Oxfordshire – was set up and new premises were found for production. The bike was promoted by the local newspaper, The Witney Gazette, and taken to various venues during 1966 including the Institution of Electrical Engineers and the London Earls Court Motorcycle Show.

A 'green' journey to work!

As the car was so novel it was featured in the December 1965 BBC Tomorrow's World programme. At the same time the Winn City Bike was also being developed – this consisted of a monocoque glass-fibre body housing a 12 volt battery and motor topped with a single seat and all running on two small spoked wheels. It was small – 42" long x 20" high x 9½" wide, it could travel up to 30mph with a 16 stone rider and the 1.2 KWH battery had a range of 10 – 20 miles. Unfortunately it was very heavy and would have taken two average people to lift the bike from the boot of the car.

Brochures were printed that stated 'Winn City Bike, all electric, no noise, no fumes' and 'It's electric, it's a winner.' Pictures showed gentlemen in their blazers and sports caps and young ladies straight from the hairdressers showing a lot of leg all sitting astride the electric bike. No one seemed to be riding it. The works destructive tester did find that after hard riding the rear wheel popped out of its locators in the glass-fibre body and also the front forks could become loose – but that was his job.

No doubt these problems were overcome and the brochure did state 'As we are continually improving the model we reserve the right to modify the specification.' [This was not the first electric bike, the first one was shown at the 1946 'Britain Can Make It Exhibition', it was designed by Benjamin Bowden and stored downhill energy to assist with up hill travel – the shape of the machine is still futuristic today.]

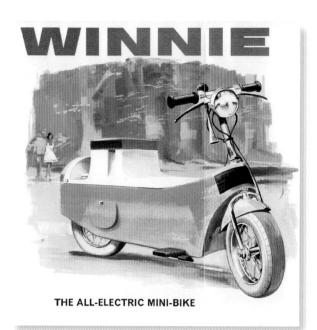

THE ALL-ELECTRIC MINI-BIKE

The down under Winnie bike.

Plenty of room for the Australian beer.

Unfortunately, sales of the Winn City Bike were poor and it is thought that production never reached three figures – by mid 1968 the company was declared bankrupt. Some of the bikes did find their way to the USA and others to Australia where the Winn City Bike renamed Winnie was still on sale in the early 1970s.

This was a bold project in the early 1960s and one that has still not been solved fifty years later. Unlike the British motorcyle industry that were too late off

the mark with scooter production, Mr Winn with his genuine attempt at something novel and pollution free was unfortunately too early for success.

The 1966 Winn City Bike in the collection is in fair original condition apart from the top plastic section that has recently been remade in small numbers for collectors of this small electric bike.

TECHNICAL DATA

YEAR	1966
ENGINE	12v electric motor
GEARBOX	Single speed
SUSPENSION	Front – rigid Rear – rigid
POWER	1.2 KWH
TOP SPEED	30 mph
COST (1966)	£104.10.0
CONDITION	Original – with new plastic top

ARIEL 3
1970-71

"Went for a ride to see if it would go over 30 m.p.h. and to establish if it would fall over"

The tilting tricycle was designed by George Wallis (brother of Barnes Wallis who invented the Dam Buster Bouncing Bomb in World War Two) at his company G L Wallis & Son of Surrey.

A prototype was built to prove the principle of the two rear wheels remaining in the vertical position while the front of the machine would lean on the bends as a conventional two-wheeler. George Wallis worked with the BSA Group and a number of three-wheeler Tina tilting trucks were made, these were used around the factory but never went into production.

Ariel four- stroke Pixie produced until the mid 1960s.

'With it' teenagers, leather clad bikers, housewives and grannies all love the Ariel 3?

Ariel Motorcycles were part of the BSA Group – the last large Ariel motorcycles were built in 1960, and their lightweight machines including the fully enclosed Ariel Leader and the small four-stroke Pixie were produced until the mid 1960s.

However, the Ariel name was revived in 1970 when the launch of the amazing Ariel 3 took place in front of the motorcycle Press at a posh Hotel in Heathrow. Obviously much market research had taken place and the Board of the BSA Group could see a brilliant future for the new machine. Was it a scooter or was it a moped? no, it was the Ariel 3 a small tilting tricycle with a 49cc engine and pedals.

The motorcycle Press had another cup of tea and then went for a ride to see if it would go over 30mph and to establish if it would fall over. They were not impressed, no one was impressed.

What to do when a new product does not impress, and the factory is ready to produce 2000 machines a week. Get demonstrator machines to all the dealers and print thousands of bold brochures showing 'with-it' teenagers, leather clad bikers, housewives and grannies all ready to take to three wheels. Maybe the slogan 'Here it is, whatever it is' didn't help! The must have extras were tinted screen, jazzy mirrors and a wire box on the back for shopping.

The Ariel 3 has a pressed steel frame, three pressed steel wheels with 12" x 2" tyres, a 49cc Dutch built moped engine with automatic transmission and centrifugal clutch, plus front and rear suspension.

This could all be purchased in Bushfire orange, Everglade green or Pacific blue for £100. Unfortunately by the end of 1971 the 'brilliant future' for the Ariel 3 came to an end – it is reported that about 4,500 were made but only a few hundred sold in the UK. George Wallis retained the patent for the tilting tricycle and in the 1980s Honda produced its Stream with a 50cc engine – this was a much improved machine but again only had a short life.

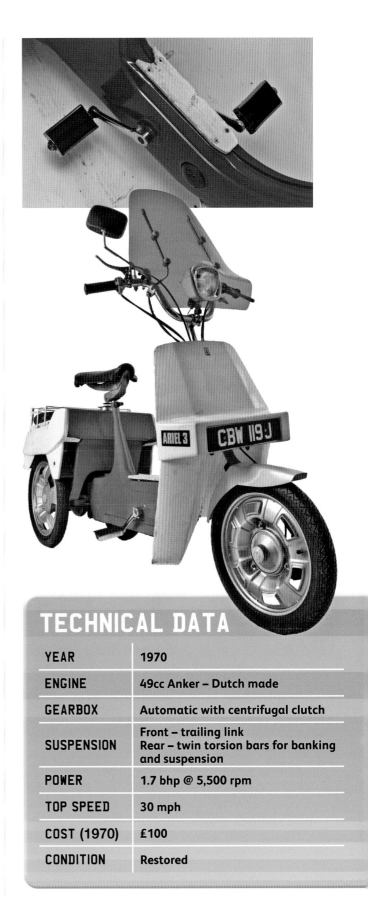

Here it is, whatever it is?

The 1970 Bushfire orange Ariel 3 in the collection has been restored and includes the attractive tinted screen. There is now a museum for Ariel 3s in the Bristol area (www.ariel3.com).

TECHNICAL DATA

YEAR	1970
ENGINE	49cc Anker – Dutch made
GEARBOX	Automatic with centrifugal clutch
SUSPENSION	Front – trailing link Rear – twin torsion bars for banking and suspension
POWER	1.7 bhp @ 5,500 rpm
TOP SPEED	30 mph
COST (1970)	£100
CONDITION	Restored

LAMBRETTA GB

View of the Italian Lambretta assembly line in 1958.

Ferdinando Innocenti was born in Italy in 1891 and set up his own steel piping company in 1926. He designed one of the first tubular scaffolding systems as well as specialising in water sprinkler systems. The company moved to the Lambrate area of Milan in 1933 and during World War Two manufactured shell cases and frames for aircraft hangers.

A fully restored 1958 Lambretta LD.

The factory was bombed in 1945 but completely rebuilt by 1948. Immediately after the War using their steel piping expertise the company designed and produced a 125cc motor scooter as transport for the masses, the Lambretta model A was shown at the 1947 Paris Show. The model A had no side panels and very limited weather protection at the front. Design improvements took place on the B and C models but they maintained the original basic shape, however, in 1951 the Lambretta LC (L for Lusso or Luxury) was introduced with side panels and full front legshields to equal the weather protection of the Vespa that had been manufactured by the Italian Piaggio company since 1946.

In Britain James and Peter Agg's Businesses included finance, hire purchase and French wines, however, a bad debt took James and his son Peter into the scooter business with the sale of a number of Lambrettas. Following a visit to Innocenti in Milan the Aggs returned as Concessionaires for Britain, the Isle of Man and Gibralter. Some of their first sales were from car showrooms as motorcycle dealers saw the Lambretta as a toy, the Aggs then made approaches to a number of British motorcycle companies to make the Lambretta under licence, like the Douglas company made the Vespa, however, they were shown the door and told they would not begin to be interested.

To make a success of selling the scooter it was realised that service centres with trained staff, recovery vehicles and spare parts would be necessary. The dealer vans were required to have the name Lambretta on them and there was also a requirement to provide rider training at the point of sale. All these requirements by Lambretta Concessionaires Ltd (established in 1951) were new to the industry and soon sales were rapidly increasing and more motorcycle dealers wanted to sell the Lambretta scooter. As time went on 1,000 service stations were made available for Lambretta owners and a dual control Lambretta scooter was developed to assist with rider training.

Soon Lambretta owners were forming clubs for runs, rallies and competitions.

From this the BLOA (British Lambretta Owners Association) and later the LCGB (Lambretta Club of Great Britain) were set up and managed by the Concessionaires – many Lambretta riders had the pleasure of seeing James or Peter Agg presenting awards at Rallies and Competitions. The Lambretta scooter arrived in the country from Italy in knockdown form so the Concessionaires were responsible for the assembly, and in addition designing the many accessories the scooters required for full weather protection, luggage carrying and enhancements to the machines.

The Lambretta Rallymaster made for the serious rally riders by the Trojan Engineering Division.

Newsletters were sent to the clubs and owner associations so information on improvements and new models plus the many accessories produced was quickly made available to riders so generating more business for the Concessionaires. The British rider was very keen on rallies and wanted more power from their Lambrettas so the Aggs were the influence that led Innocenti to increase the engine size from 150 to 175cc in the TV175 scooter that appeared in 1957. In 1959 the amalgamation of Lambretta Concessionaires and the Trojan Engineering Company of Croydon, Surrey took place and the Lambretta business was moved from Wimbledon to the Croydon site.

Two years later a British Lambretta was developed to meet the needs of the rally riders. The Rallymaster scooter was based on a standard Li series 2 machine with a second stage rally conversion to the 150cc engine carried out by the Trojan Engineering Division.

The fixed front mudguard of the Standard Li was replaced with a turning mudguard used on Spanish Lambrettas, the special machine also incorporated a dualseat, spot lamp, spare wheel behind the legshields topped with a dashboard including rev counter, stop watch holder and map reading lamp. The Rallymaster was also fitted with a sports type Perspex screen, GB plate, rally number plates and a lifting handle at the rear.

All these modifications had been suggested by the top rally riders of the time. To further enhance the scooter the standard red or blue side panels were painted with four black horizontal stripes. This was a striking looking machine and assisted Lambretta to continue winning awards in many of the popular rallies including the Welsh three-day trial and the Isle of Man scooter rally. The Rallymaster had a top speed of 55mph and was listed in 1961 at £183.15.0 against the standard Li 150 at £159.17.6 and the TV175 at £179.17.6. It has been reported that 140 of the British modified Lambrettas were made by Trojan.

The company Trojan Ltd was registered in 1914 as a precision and general engineering company.

After the Second World War Trojan produced a new 15cwt van.

The company was immediately involved in the war effort but continued the development of a basic and inexpensive car using a two-stroke engine with chain drive and solid tyres. The company moved to Croydon, Surrey in 1927 and began production of a commercial delivery van. After the Second World War they produced a new 15 cwt van and in 1947 began the manufacture of the Piatti designed Mini-Motor with a 49cc two-stroke engine positioned above the rear bicycle wheel and driving the wheel with a roller on the tyre.

The engine was also used for lawn mowers, stationary engines and vacuum pumps for milking – also a 75cc engine was produced for commercial tricycles and other uses. It is stated between 1947 and 1956 some 75,000 units were made.

Following the take-over in 1959 Lambretta/Trojan were assembling the Lambretta scooter and later making the Rallymaster and scooter box sidecars plus the Trokart, Trobike and then the Trojan 200 Bubblecar.

Trojan/Heinkel Bubblecars at the German Scooter Rally in Lincolnshire 2010.

This vehicle was based on the Heinkel made in Germany from 1956 to 1959. The rights were then sold to Dundalk Engineering of Ireland who continued production until 1961 when Trojan started to make the car. Five models were made including three and four wheelers and a three wheel van.

The production of the Bubblecar replaced the manufacture of the famous 15cwt van that the company had made since the late 1940s. 12,000 Trojan Bubblecars were built between 1961-1965. In the early 1960s Trojan also bought the Elva

Sports Car company and began the manufacture of the Elva Courier and Elva Racing Cars. Later the company teamed with McLaren to build McLaren racing cars, and using this experience Trojan went on to build their own Formula 1 car which it raced in 1974.

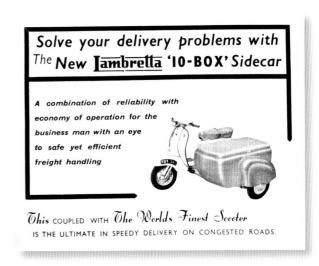

Solve your delivery problems with The New **lambretta** '10-BOX' Sidecar

A combination of reliability with economy of operation for the business man with an eye to safe yet efficient freight handling

This COUPLED WITH *The World's Finest Scooter* IS THE ULTIMATE IN SPEEDY DELIVERY ON CONGESTED ROADS.

Following the success of Lambretta Concessionaires in persuading Innocenti to manufacture the TV175 they again succeeded with the introduction of the TV200 known in Britain as the GT200, this was further improved in 1969 as the Grand Prix 200. In the late 1960s the Concessionaires had assisted Innocenti in being given the right to use the British Mini engine for a similar size Innocenti car. Innocenti at this time were having industrial relations and financial problems and this allowed the British Leyland Motor Corporation to buy the company. Unfortunately BLMC decided to stop the manufacture of all Lambretta scooters and the whole manufacturing equipment was sold to India. The last Lambretta scooter came off the production line in April 1971. A number of Spanish Lambrettas were imported to Britain by Lambretta/Trojan but this was not a success.

By this time Lambretta/Trojan were importing the Japanese Suzuki motorcycles using their previous set up and dealer network and later formed their own racing team Heron Suzuki employing world champion racer Barry Sheene.

When the Douglas company stopped importing Italian Vespas in 1982, Trojan took over this work for a while but this again was not a success.

The Lambretta good life of the late 1950s.

One of Peter Agg's later projects was displaying his collection of fine vehicles including the Trojan Bubblecar at a Restaurant with a large dance floor at Effingham Park near Crawley, Surrey.

Although the Lambretta club of Great Britain went through some low times in the 1970/80s the club is now thriving again with the aim of promoting Lambretta lifestyle and preservation of the machines.

A Trojan Bubblecar, made between 1961 to 1965.

Will the club now have a further high with the announcement in 2011 that a new twist and go metal bodied Lambretta – taking design lines from the 1963 Li Slim Line Special – is now in the showrooms and about to unite Lambretta and GB once again. Also, there is now a Trojan Museum Trust – set up to acquire old vehicles made by Trojan – with Peter Agg as its Patron. (Sadly the Trust announced the death of Peter Agg, at the age of 82, in March 2012.)

The new Lambretta LN125 twist and go scooter.

BRITISH SCOOTER PROTOTYPES NOT IN THE COLLECTION

BSA DINGHY (1940s)

The first American scooter made following the Great Depression was the Salsbury Motor Glide of 1935. During the Second World War the American Cushman model 53 Airbourne scooter was seen on many airstrips around the world. The sight of this military scooter gave birth to a number of post-war scooters including the Innocenti Lambretta A, the Japanese Fuji Rabbit and the British Swallow Gadabout, and no doubt a prototype Dinghy scooter made by the BSA Company in the early 1940s.

BSA Dinghy prototype with Mr Graham Walker editor of Motorcycling magazine, VMCC archives.

This machine looked very similar to the 1939 Salsbury – and is shown in Bert Hopwood's book 'Whatever happened to the British Motorcycle Industry', the book shows a smart dark coloured scooter with the BSA badge on the side with the Managing Director's secretary Gwen Arey sitting on the machine showing her 1940s' fashions. The Dinghy pictured shows the editor of the Motorcycling magazine, Mr Graham Walker, sitting on a prototype – this may be a second prototype as it has full legshields and a larger headlamp compared with the Gwen Arey's scooter.

The machine was designed by Erling Poppe and given the name Dinghy, it had a side valve four-stroke engine with semi-automatic transmission. Erling Poppe worked with the BSA design team during the war years, his Dinghy project reached the prototype stage but unfortunately never went into production. Another of his projects was the Sunbeam S7 motorcycle, this was a gentleman's machine with a 487cc in-line twin engine and a shaft drive. The gentleman's machine sold from 1946 for ten years and was improved in 1949 as the S8. What a pity the ladie's machine, the Dinghy scooter, was not developed, the Dinghy would have found its place next to the Corgi and Swallow Gadabout and if developed into a fully automatic transmission would have allowed BSA to lead the 1950s scooter boom instead of waiting until 1958 when the BSA Sunbeam scooter was announced.

Another interesting picture in Bert Hopwood's book is a lightweight machine which is captioned as 'An early BSA moped of the late 1930s which did not reach production.' The name moped of course was not used until the mid 1950s, this machine was no doubt an early Autocycle introduced after the Budget change in 1931 giving a road tax reduction to motorcycles under 150cc. It looks an improvement on what became the standard design for an Autocycle, were these two small machines two big opportunities missed by the BSA Group?

RIDLEY ELECTRIC SCOOTER (1948)

Following World War Two many people were looking for a cheap form of personal transport. Mr C.V.Ridley, a motor engineer from Coventry, decided the way forward was to do it yourself. From his garage full of ancient car bits he spent many evenings building an electric scooter from spare parts including a car chassis and even a steering wheel to be used instead of the conventional bike handlebars.

The scooter was powered by a 12 volt battery through a starter motor and bevel-drive to the rear wheel. The machine could reach speeds of 30 mph with a range of 12 miles on one battery charge, this made the scooter extremely cheap to run – but Mr Ridley still planned to further reduce the operating costs by building a wind driven dynamo to recharge the battery. The most difficult part of the work to enable the scooter to be used on the road was dealing with the licencing authority, proving the spares parts used were not from stolen cars, and establishing a classification for an electric scooter with a steering wheel!

Thankfully this rare machine has survived and is now in the Coventry Transport Museum. It would be the mid 1960s before another engineer produced an electric scooter called the Winn City Bike and the Twenty-First century before other manufacturers successfully made electric scooters and the wind turbines to satisfy Mr Ridley's 1948 dream.

Bits and pieces making an electric scooter before its time.

CAIRN (1950)

In 1950 – during the Brockhouse Corgi production period – a Mr Farrow of Reading designed and built a scooter in the Corgi style called a Cairn with full metal enclosure of the steel frame, tank and engine.

Mr Farrow's Corgi style bike with full engine enclosure.

The machine had small disc wheels with cycle mudguards, no legshields or footboards, no suspension, adjustable handlebars and saddle, and vents within the enclosure to assist cooling of the 98cc Villiers engine. A rear carrier, pannier frames and twin rear lights were incorporated in the design along with speed flashes and the Cairn name fixed on the engine covers. It was a streamlined design that would have protected the rider from engine dirt and it was reported to have a satisfactory ride as a runabout. No doubt the difficulties of moving from a prototype to production stopped the Cairn from moving forward. A few years later another totally enclosed Corgi style machine designed by the Italian Vincenti Piatti would be a little more successful.

COMMANDER (1952)

At the time when all Autocycles and most lightweight motorcycles looked somewhat basic a machine called the Commander was displayed at the 1952 London Earls Court Show that looked like something from the future. Three different models were shown all using the same frame made of square sectioned tubing and covered by flowing steel pressings with a large chrome plated grill enclosing the engine. Front suspension was leading-link forks using rubber bands and the rear was a pivoted fork with a coil spring.

Three machines from the future that unfortunately did not reach production.

The machine's handlebars and cables were completely covered and the two levers were hinged from the bar ends, the smart headlamp was positioned just below the handlebars and shaped to blend in with the front of the bike.

The Commander looked like something from the future.

The Commander I model was listed as an Autocycle with a Villiers 98cc single speed unit and was given the normal Autocycle pedals. Listed as

an ultra lightweight motorcycle the Commander II used the Villiers 98cc two speed engine, and the top of the range III had the 122cc Villiers engine with a three speed gearbox. A long list of extras were available and the Commander III on the stand had legshields, footboards and a windscreen making it a very attractive scooterette. Prices ranged from £75 to £95 and marketing was by the General Steel Group of Hayes, Middlesex, part of EMI who were already selling the Cyclemaster cyclemotor.

Their advertising claimed '3 revolutionary machines powered by Villiers. Modern low cost motoring in armchair comfort', an optional dualseat was available and three two-tone paint jobs enhanced the machines. The Commanders were modern, revolutionary and so different for an early post-war machine – no doubt they were a sensation at the Show. Potential buyers had to wait a few months until a further brief reference was made in April 1953 – after which they were never heard of again.

OSCAR (1953)

In late 1952 Lawrie Bond sold the design of his BAC Gazelle scooter to a company called Projects and Developments Ltd of Blackburn, Lancashire. Although the new owners made a few improvements the scooter never reached the production stage. However, one of Bond's engineering staff did move to Projects and Developments to work on a totally new scooter. The new machine called the Oscar was first shown

at the German Frankfurt show in 1953 and then at the London Earls Court show a few weeks later. The Oscar was the centre of attraction with it's elegant streamlined body made of glass-fibre, some of the design work on the scooter had been undertaken by the project engineer's wife who was a professional industrial designer.

The machine had many novel features; as well as being the first scooter with a glass-fibre bodywork it had rubber in tension suspension, linked brakes, a very quiet exhaust using perforated sheet metal and glass wool and a hand start on the smaller engine.

THE BRITISH DESIGNED AND BUILT "OSCAR" has—

★ **Accommodation** for two persons on a comfortable dual seat. Space for two large suitcases and all are well protected from weather and mud

★ **Silence and Smoothness** which is remarkable; achieved by an exclusive design of exhaust silencer together with resilient rubber mounting of the entire engine, and exhaust system.

★ **Exceptional Stability and Safety** ensured by the use of specially large wheels rigidly mounted on both sides to supple rubber suspension units.

★ **Outstanding Non-skid** characteristics built into the design by unique suspension and correctly proportioned braking between front and rear wheels.

★ **Both Road Wheels** interchangeable and easily removed by a single bolt without disturbing either final drive chain or brakes. A cushion drive is provided.

★ **Beauty** of Line, Accessibility, and is easily cleaned.

"OSCAR" IS ON STAND 52 AT EARLS COURT.

PROJECTS & DEVELOPMENTS LTD., BLACKBURN, ENGLAND

Two Villiers engine sizes were available a 122cc three speed with a 6 volt system and an extendable hand start positioned on the right hand footboard, and a 197cc three speed with a 12 volt battery and an electric start. Both engines were fitted with a Villiers fan unit attached to the flywheel. These were the first British scooters to have a fan cooled engine. By undoing two quick action fasteners the rear body hinged forward for access to the engine, rear wheel and chain. The dualseat had a lock operated by the ignition key giving access to the filler cap and a small storage space.

Body hinged forward to access Villiers fan cooled engine.

The footbrake on the left hand side of the footboards operated both front and rear brakes, however, a conventional lever on the handlebars could still be used to operate just the front brake. The gear change was undertaken by two toe pedals on the right hand side – this was just one of the features to assist lady riders.

Although the glass-fibre body was a first [apart from the strange roofed machine taken to the Sahara by 'Spike' Rhiando] it was stated that steelwork may be used on production runs. The projected cost of the Oscar was £149.8.0 for the 125cc and £159.0.0 for the 200cc. At the time a Lambretta 125D was £139.17.6 and a Zundapp Bella 150 was £180. Unfortunately, even with the elegant lines, novel specification and competitive prices the Oscar never went into production, this was a big missed opportunity for the British scooter industry.

It is thought maybe six prototype scooters were made, some for the German Show and some for the London show.

One 197cc Oscar was used in the late 1950s as a mobile test bed for the British company Siba Electric Ltd., based near Camberley in Surrey, for development of their 'Dynastart' electric start for scooters and motorcycles. However, only two and some spare parts are known to survive – both with the 197cc units and electric starter motor – and both are safe with scooter collectors in Britain.

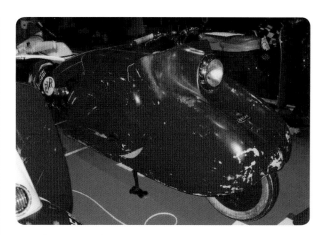

Rare Oscar at a VMSC show.

HARPER SCOOTOMOBILE (1954 – 56)

A number of scooter manufacturers used different tests and stunts to prove their scooters reliability including riding up mountains, 24 hour trials, and of course Lands End to John o' Groats runs. However, only one designer decided to ride his prototype scooter to Cape Town in South Africa via the Sahara Desert. The scooter was the Saharan and the designer Alvin 'Spike' Rhiando.

'Spike' Rhiando was born in Canada to a circus family and did his time as a trapeze artist, his adventurous lifestyle led him to motorcycle rodeos and midget car racing. Following limited success in racing 'Spike' turned his attention to designing a scooter and – due to other business interests – promoted the use of GRP (Glass Reinforced

Plastic) for the bodywork of the scooter. The GRP body was designed to totally enclose the machine including a built in windscreen and a roof to protect from the scorching sun when tackling the Sahara desert. The 197cc Villiers engine had a car type electric starter, hand gear change and was equipped with two cooling fans.

'Spike' Rhiando with his Saharan with glass-fibre body, twin fan cooled engine and roof for protection from the sun.

The ride to Cape Town began on the 3rd January 1953, obviously hardships were expected along the route, however, conditions were far worse than planned. Deep snow had fallen in the foothills of the Atlas Mountains, strong winds and sandstorms were experienced in the Sahara Desert – and there was no back-up vehicle to assist. After approximately 800 miles in first gear through snow and soft sand the prototype Saharan scooter decided to retire. After some very cold nights on his own 'Spike' fortunately was rescued, and at a later date some of the scooter was also returned home. But, with 2,500 miles of the daring trip accomplished he had gained valuable experiential learning for the planning stages of the next phase of his scooter project.

'Spike' on the elegant glass-fibre Harper Scootomobile.

Developing the Saharan into a road scooter took 'Spike' to Devon and a working relationship with the Harper Aircraft Co. Ltd. of Exeter who at the time in 1953 where producing huge aircraft parts for the early V-bombers (the Valiant, Vulcan and Victor). 'Spikes' design ideas for the new scooter were turned into detailed engineering drawings by Harper's aeronautical engineer Mr Keys. The scooter, to be known as the Scootomobile, used a space frame much modified from the original shape used on the Saharan, the front suspension was by telescopic forks and the brochure quotes the rear suspension as 'Patented Lamibar rear suspension comprising a specially developed laminated torsion bar. This gives a total possible rear wheel movement of 7½". This form of suspension sets a new standard in rider comfort.'

Initially the engine was either a 122cc or 197cc Villiers unit but the scooter brochure only lists the 197cc. The de luxe model included a self starter motor using a rubber belt to turn the flywheel magneto. The bodywork – using experience from the Saharan – was of course glass-fibre with a built in windscreen and twin rear panniers. The bodywork included a door behind the legshields to access the battery, and the engine could be reached by lifting the foam rubber dualseat. The brochure quoted 'The complete rear body shell hinges upwards at the rear to expose all the mechanism.' The wheels used were steel rimmed with cast aluminium hubs housing 6" diameter brakes. Tyres were 3.50 or 4.00 x 12".

The Motor Cycling review tester stated the scooters stability 'was little short of amazing' and on road holding 'neither rider nor passenger had anything but praise'. The review finished by saying 'It is expected that the first production models will come off the assembly lines within the next few months.'

The Motor Cycling magazines review on the 4th November 1954 stated that minor changes had been made to the bodywork – the nose section had been given more flowing lines – and the space frame had been redesigned. It stated that the scooter was now in production and would be seen at the forthcoming London Earls Court Show.

[What it did not state was that Harper had bought the Stanley Engineering Company of Egham, Surrey and in July 1954 started production of the Harper Invalid Carriage. This carriage had a full glass-fibre body and was powered by either a 36 volt electric motor or the 197cc Villiers engine.]

Two Harper Scootomobiles were at the 1954 show fitted with front and rear chrome bumpers, bright metal strips on the body and attractive whitewall tyres (the brochure shows these items as extras). The November 1955 Power and Pedal magazine stated 'Not at the show, but on the

British market in 1956 – the Harper Scootomobile'. A single page brochure was prepared and quoted 'Scootomobile, The Finest machine on two wheels, Armchair comfort: complete protection: Indestructible Bodywork: Electric Self Starter' – with the 197cc engine the price given was £175.13.0. Unfortunately all this was not to be – the Scootomobile failed to go into full production. In 1961 four remaining pre-production scooters were eventually sold to company employees including one to a 17 year old engineering apprentice Mike Naish at the amazing price of £52. A very lucky lad.

The February 1959 Power and Pedal magazine under its 'comment by Clip-on' section showed a picture of the Harper with the caption 'The Harper "Scootomobile" as shown at Earls Court in 1954. Only six of these machines were made but a single more elaborate edition appeared at the London Plastics exhibition in the following year.' Clip-on once again praised the handling of the scooter, 'I rode the machine on the track at Exeter airport, an atrocious surface with cracks several inches wide across it in places. Even on this stuff the Harper handled very well and it was while I was demonstrating its stability to myself by riding side saddle and with my arms folded that I was passed at some 50mph by Rhiando on another model standing up and controlling the scooter by two fingers of one hand resting on the top of the screen.'

Rhiando's son Max continued the glass-fibre business with a scooter theme by selling a range of luggage accessories under the name Rhiando Products of Guildford Surrey. The range was designed for the Italian Lambretta, Vespa and Iso scooters and included the Scootokaddy mounted over the front mudguard, the Handykaddy positioned behind the legshields and the Kaddyettes as a pair of rear panniers. These were introduced in 1959 and sold into the early 1960s.

INVEST IN THE BEST

BUY "FULLY GUARANTEED" RHIANDO "RHITEGLASS" EQUIPMENT

" SCOOTOKADDY "
RETAIL PRICE £9. 19. 6.
(illustrated)
DE LUXE £12. 0. 0. (with locks)
● LOCK EXTRA - 2 KEYS 17/6
● MATCHING COLOURS
● SPACIOUS CONTAINERS
FOR ALL

"HANDYKADDY"
RETAIL PRICE £3. 19. 6. each

LAMBRETTA · VESPA · ISO
AND OTHER MODELS
SEE YOUR DEALER OR WRITE FOR BROCHURE
RHIANDO PRODUCTS
219 STOUGHTON ROAD · GUILDFORD · SURREY
REGD. DESIGN AND PATENT APPLIED FOR.

" KADDYETTES "
RETAIL PRICE £3. 12. 6. (illustrated)
£2. 19. 6.

Max Rhiando's scooter luggage containers in Rhiteglass.

Harpers went on to produce improved Invalid Carriages winning contracts to build standard specification carriages for the Ministry of Health until closure in 1965. Furthermore, Stanley Engineering were sole concessionaires for German Adler motorcycles in 1956 and early 1957 including the Adler 98cc Junior scooter. So, the Harper Group did sell a scooter but what a shame it was not the 197cc streamlined Scootomobile designed by 'Spike' Rhiando based on his experience in the Sahara Desert.

However, one Scootomobile does remain in restored condition in the Haynes Museum Somerset. The scooter was presented to the museum in pieces and with the museums skills and some original drawings the futuristic design of the Scootomobile may still be enjoyed. The model is the final design with flashing winkers – a tribute to the daring man from the circus. (www.haynesmotormuseum.com).

BSA BEEZA (1955)

The BSA Beeza scooter – in a delicate shade of blue – had a good reception at the 1955 London Earls Court Show including a photograph taken with the President of the Board of Trade (Mr Peter Thorneycroft, MP) sitting and smiling on the new scooter.

Josephine Griffen with the good looking prototype Beeza.

It was a very good looking machine – especially when film star Josephine Griffen took her turn to sit on it – and obviously BSA were proud of the specification with its single cylinder alpha-head four-stroke 198cc engine incorporating micro-babbit big end bearing and its dual exhaust systems with primary expansion chamber. Were BSA really trying to impress the buyers of scooters who were much more interested in the colour and price? The machine possessed a large horizontal tube as the main frame with engine and drive hanging from it which would have given the scooter good road holding characteristics. It also had an electric car type starter and interchangeable wheels – so a really promising specification.

Following the show the BSA Management wanted it in production as soon as possible and the January 1956 Scooter World Magazine stated 'In production date of March/April 1956'.

A good specification for a large scooter in 1955, but a long wait until 1958 before the Beeza's replacement took to the road.

The advertisement in the same magazine for Fred Warnell's Shop of Chingford Mount Road, E4 showed 'Agents for the following' – ten scooters were listed including Lambretta, Bella, Albatross and the new Beeza.

Thousands of single page leaflets were printed in November 1955 showing the attractive scooter and stating 'The Beeza a Brilliant New Scooter!' and listing all the outstanding and complex technical details. The price was shown as £204-12-0, this was the same price as the German Zundapp Bella 200, three pounds cheaper than the Dayton Albatross 225cc and £43 cheaper than the four-stroke German Heinkel Tourist which at that time was being imported by the Excelsior Motorcycle Company. So, good looking, high specification and right price – what went wrong?

In the December 1956 issue of Scooter World there was a sad little note, 'BSA Motorcycles Ltd. have decided not to go ahead immediately with their luxury model, the 200cc four-stroke Beeza.' It went on to mention increased labour and material costs, uncompetitive in price in overseas markets, and that the scooter will not go into production as intended.

Nowhere amongst the vast technical data given on the Beeza can the brake horse power of the four-stroke side valve engine be found – no one wants to spend a lot of money on a 200cc luxury touring scooter to be overtaken by a cheaper 150cc machine. Also, further price increases would put it in direct competition with one of the best four-stroke scooters in the world made by Professor Heinkel.

The BSA Group would have to wait a few more years until the Triumph 'Speed Twin' designer Edward Turner brought another four-stroke scooter to the British market.

PULLIN (1955)

At the age of 21 Cyril Pullin won the Senior TT in 1914 on a Rudge Multi at an average speed of approximately 49mph. Over the next 40 years Pullin would be involved in motorcycle design work including a motorcycle of advanced design using a pressed steel frame with an enclosed engine. The Ascot-Pullin introduced in 1928 used a 496cc horizontal overhead valve engine with a three speed hand change gearbox and interconnected hydraulic brakes.

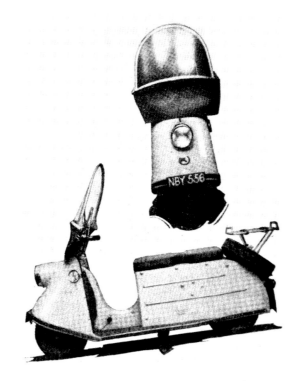

The Pullin Pony waiting in vain for a interested manufacturer. Mortons Archive.

Unfortunately very few were sold due to the high cost, a low top speed and a few handling problems, production ceased in 1930.

In 1951 Pullin designed a very complex rotary engine as an in-wheel cyclemotor, a working prototype model was built but the little motor never reached production.

1955 saw the production of his prototype scooter. Gone were his advanced design trends – this was a machine that could easily be produced by a small company with limited workshop facilities. The front and rear body used simple single curvature bends eliminating the need for costly press tools, the rear suspension was swinging arm and the front leading link. The Pullin Pony used

the 197cc Villiers engine with an electric start, and an emergency detachable kick start was also included.

The interchangeable wheels were 8" diameter with 6" brakes. The scooter had a dualseat with spare wheel, rear carrier and luggage pockets behind the legshields – a screen completed the rider's full protection.

Unable to progress the project himself Pullin wanted a manufacturer to take his design forward into production. 1955 was definitely the time to promote such a machine with very little competition on the market, but neither small companies nor the British motorcycle industry were interested so unfortunately the project never got past the prototype stage.

REYNOLDS SCOOTERETTE (1956)

The Reynolds family business started making nails in 1841 at their factory in Birmingham, by 1889 they were making tubes for the new bicycle industry and had a new company name 'The Patent Butted Tube Company'. In 1923 the company name was changed to Reynolds Tube Company Ltd and in 1928 they voluntarily joined the Tube Investment Group.

As a result of their experience making high quality tube for aeroplanes during World War One they went on to manufacture the famous 531 tubing in 1935. In the 1950s Reynolds were designing and making frames for many British mopeds and scooters including Dayton, Dunkley and DKR.

1956 Reynolds Dunelt Moped.

During this period the company decided to design and make a number of frames for mopeds / scooterettes including front and rear suspension and fittings for proprietary engines.

At the 1956 London Earls Court Show a moped was shown using one of these frames with a 49cc German Victoria two-stroke engine and a two speed gearbox. The moped was showing the name Dunelt – this was a motorcycle company who made machines from 1919 to 1935 – a name owned by Tube Investments. The moped did not go into production and the Reynolds designed frame was not taken up by other manufacturers. At this time the large Villiers Company did not make a 50cc moped engine, so the low volume JAP (J.A.Prestwick) or a Continental suppliers engine would have to be used.

It would therefore have been easier for British manufacturers to import Continental mopeds (with a little badge engineering) as successfully undertaken by Kieft, Norman and Bown.

As well as the Dunelt moped another prototype machine was made and used on the road – this time a scooterette. It is believed Reynolds named this scooterette the Dunelt No-ped, the machine had a Villiers 98cc engine with a kickstart instead of moped pedals. It looks to have a very similar frame to the moped with front and rear suspension, but with scooter style legshields, footboards and complete engine enclosures. The engine had a two speed hand change gearbox, and the handlebars were covered with a smart cowling including a speedo.

The Reynolds Dunelt No-Ped.

The Reynolds Dunelt No-Ped in 2012.

The No-ped which still exists is missing the engine enclosures, and modifications have been made to the ignition coil and saddle. It is a good looking small machine and would have competed well with the BSA Dandy and small Mercury and Dunkley scooters. Efforts were made by Reynolds to sell these frames/machines by displays at both Cycle and Motorcycle Shows but they remained just prototypes. However, without Reynolds high quality tubing and their frame design work – accommodating British Villiers engines of course

– there would have been little to choose between if wishing to buy a British scooter in the 1950s/60s.

PROGRESS SUPREME (1957/58)

Progress scooters were produced in Germany from 1953 and sold in Britain from 1956 to 1958. The scooter was a big machine with 16" spoked wheels a long wheel base, and used the 191cc Sachs engine. It had a kick or electric start, a large headlamp which turned with the front wheel and a novel neutral selector lever on the handlebars. It was the most expensive scooter at the time and one of the fastest and due to its large wheels the machine handled more like a motorcycle than a conventional scooter.

The fine German Progress scooter with a 191cc Sachs engine.

The scooters were imported into Britain by a long standing garage business Carr Bros. of Purley, Surrey, who also imported the Italian Parilla Greyhound scooter with a 150cc engine.

Two Progress scooters were imported, the 200 Continental with a four speed Sachs 191cc engine with electric start at £254.4.0, and the 200 Major with a kick start at £215.15.3 – a luggage carrier was available as an extra. Carr Bros. had similar ideas about the imported Progress scooters as Cyril Kieft did about his imported German Hercules scooter.

The British Progress scooter with a Villiers engine at the 1956 London Earls Court Show.

The idea being to replace the Sachs unit with a British Villiers engine and produce a lower cost machine with cheaper and readily available engines and spares. Cyril Kieft went on to manufacture the successful range of DKR scooters, however Carr Bros. decided to use Villiers engines and build a similar looking glass-fibre body for the German scooter and sell the scooter under the Progress name.

The Progress–Supreme Company (a subsidiary of Carr Bros.) was proud to present for 1957 the following programme in addition to their German imported machines – a Progress 200 Britannia with a Villiers 197cc engine with four speeds, fan cooling and an electric self starter. They stated the machine had attractive styling, was fully equipped and had a crimson red glass-fibre body. The cost was £204.12.0 plus £20 extra if the German Sachs wheels with 5½ brakes were required. (The standard wheels had Dunlop rims with 5¼" brakes by British Hubs.)

The British Progress Tourette three wheeler was the cheapest microcar of the time.

The Progress 200 Briton had the same engine but a three speed box and kickstart, this had a standard colour of Blue-Green and cost £186.12.5. The third scooter was the 150 Anglian using a 147cc Villiers fan cooled engine with three speeds at a cost of just £174.16.5. The Anglian was given the colour of Saxe-Blue but all machines could be ordered in any colour for an extra £5. All three scooters had a welded tubular frame with pivoted fork suspension front and rear.

In the Scooter World magazine dated December 1956 under the heading 'Impressions of Earls Court 1956' it said that the Progress-Supreme Co. had 'A fine show of the slightly re-designed Progress scooters with and without sidecars.' The three glass-fibre Villiers engine machines were shown alongside the Parilla scooter, moped and a three-wheeler car.

Down at Progress-Supreme in Purley the Panel Shop of the Carr Bros. garage had been handed over to its subsidiary to build the new scooters and microcars. Six assembly positions for the scooter and six for the car had been made available for their 1957 Business Plan. The little three wheeler car had been given the name of Tourette Supreme and was to be built from two glass-fibre sections joined at the waistline in the style of an easter egg with the single rear wheel driven by a Villiers 197cc engine. The cars would be made in various trim with cloth or plastic hoods or a glass-fibre cabin top, prices started at just £229.10.0 – the cheapest microcar on the market at that time.

Unfortunately, very few Progress-Supreme scooters were made, maybe because the costs of all three scooters began to climb and by May 1958 the British 150cc with the German wheels was more expensive than the German Progress 200cc kickstart. Manufacturing must have ceased at Carr Bros. prior to May 1959 as the Power and Pedal magazine reported 'A new company, Messers Progress and Parilla scooters of Selcroft Road, Purley, Surrey have spares for all models of these machines.' It is known that at least one complete Progress-Supreme scooter has survived but it is not known how many were built.

DOT VIVI (1957/1963)

The Dot motorcycle company was set up in 1903 by Harry Reed and located in Manchester, Harry Reed won TT races in 1904 and in the sidecar class in 1924, most of their machines were made for competition work. Following the Second World War Dot (said to mean Devoid Of Trouble) made a three wheeled motorcycle truck with a 122cc Villiers engine and then returned to mainly off-road competition motorcycles many having Villiers engines.

The DOT VIVI Scooterette is a most attractive little mount ; it is beautiful in appearance, light in weight, easy to handle, and a joy to keep clean. It gives considerable weather protection, in addition to all the other virtues of the Moped.

84 GNS. INCLUDING TAX

SPECIFICATION

FRAME.	A " one piece " deep steel pressing, of smooth contours and streamlined appearance, with a cleverly designed frontal, enclosing the engine unit and combining wet road weather protection with beauty of appearance.
SUSPENSION.	Swinging arm rear suspension with hydraulic shock absorbing units. Leading link front forks with oscillating brake plate and parallel action linkage. DOT patent 750590.
WHEELS.	24″ × 2″ with 4″ diameter internal expanding brakes.
LIGHTING.	18 watt Electric, from engine dynamo.
MUDGUARDS.	Strong, deeply formed as illustrated. Note the built-in rear guard, designed to protect the rider against mud and dust, and for easier cleanliness.
POWER UNIT.	VICTORIA 48 c.c. (2 Horse power) helical drive two speed in unit construction. Multiple plate clutch and built in pedalling gear. Detachable alloy cylinder head. All controls mounted on handle bars.
FINISH.	Modern two-tone pastel shades of Fawn and Grey.

Dot-Vivi Scooterette

The attractive Dot-Vivi scooterette with a pressed steel body and full legshields.

In 1951 a Brockhouse 248cc engine was used in a Dot machine at the same time Brockhouse were manufacturing the Corgi scooter.

To increase their range of machines Dot started to sell the Dot-Vivi 48cc machines in 1957. The three machines, a moped, a racer and a scooterette were made by Viberti of Turin Italy – manufacturers of bus and coach bodies and trailers – and fitted with two-stroke engines made by Victoria of Germany, Vivi comes from the two company names.

The Dot-Vivi brochure for the scooterette stated 'The DOT VIVI scooterette is a most attractive little mount; it is beautiful in appearance, light in weight, easy to handle, and a joy to keep clean.

An excellent restored Dot Vivi Racer at the Stafford Motor Cycle Show 2010.

It gives considerable weather protection, in addition to all the other virtues of the moped.' It was attractive with its pressed steel frame housing the tank and tool box and 'with a cleverly designed frontal, enclosing the engine unit and combining

bad weather protection with beautiful appearance.' It had suspension front and rear and a two speed gearbox all in 'modern two-tone pastel shades of Fawn and Grey.' The scooterette had 24" x 2" wheels and a deep rear mudguard to protect the rider, the engine in the scooterette and moped produced 2 brake horsepower and the racer was tuned to give 2.6.

The scooterette was shown in the scooter magazine price lists from 1957 through to 1963 at a cost of £88-4-0. This was another attempt by a British motorcycle company to have a share of the growing moped and light scooter market by importing Continental machines, it has been reported that approximately 300 Dot-Vivi machines were sold in Britain.

HOLT SHERPA (1957)

Another minimum cost solution for a scooter in 1957 came from Mr Harry Holt. Mr Holt of Ilford had given 62 years service to the motor vehicle industry, taken out 30 patents and registered designs in Britain and other countries and written various articles for the Power and Pedal magazine since its start in 1952. In 1957 he announced the Sherpa, the first British prefabricated machine having alternative 50cc or 100cc engines and variants of both moped or scooter specification.

Once the customer had chosen their specification 'it can be made in prefabricated parts assembled by bolt-up.' The first flat pack scooter!

It has all been said by Mr Holt!

A new approach to moped/scooter design by Mr Harry Holt.

An advert in the November 1957 Power and Pedal stated 'A World Leader, an all British Moped-Scooter!' It claimed charming design, perfect balance, cleanliness and lightness, it could be purchased with folding legshields and a large enclosed luggage capacity. Obviously its fabricated design was fully patented and registered and the machine had 'prospective retail prices from 60 to 100 Guineas.' The Sherpa, moped or scooter, never appeared in the Power and Pedal price list and was never heard of again. After the Bond Sherpa in 1955 this was the second time a poor Sherpa failed to reach production.

AIRSCOOTER (1958/62)

When you are a director of a company and fly light aircraft to the continent and dislike the high taxi fares abroad you look for an alternative.
Mr K.G.Willinger, a director of Industrial Plastics came up with the idea of making a lightweight scooter that could be easily dismantled and carried in his Auster aircraft. The first prototype had a four-stroke engine in a frame with no suspension – it worked but came with a lot of noise and discomfort.

Mr Bird the chief engineer of Industrial Plastics, along with the Reynold Tube Company, came up with a far superior model. The little machine called the Airscooter had front and rear suspension, dismantled to four main components in a few minutes and was powered by a 49cc Zundapp moped engine.

After the flight- off we go.

Four into one in just 3 minutes.

As well as for light aircraft the Airscooter would be ideal for carrying on boats and in car boots. Airscooter Ltd of Regent Street, London, was set up and stated they hoped to make 25 per week at the start of 1958 increasing to 50 per week by the year end. Two models would be made – a single speed one at £105 and a two speed one at £113, it was hoped to reduce these prices when production got underway.

The scooter was in the magazine price lists from early 1958 to mid 1962 as a two speed model and priced for the whole period at £105-5-0. The Airscooter was not the only folding scooter, the French made the Martin-Moulet machine that folded into a luggage case, and this was made under licence in the USA called the Foldmobile. Obviously those abroad also thought the black cab fares in London were too high.

One Airscooter was seen at a British Motorcycle Show some time ago but it is not known how many were made or if any others survived. Maybe somewhere in a shed or cellar a little pile of bits could be ridden off as a scooter in just three minutes.

The box section cross-bar split the unit in two and the dualseat and handlebars made up the four components. The cross-bar slotted together and was held in place with a wing nut and the whole assembly took less than three minutes.

POWELL JOYBIKE SCOOTERETTE (1958)

Shown below is a trade news item from the August 1958 Power and Pedal magazine announcing a new all British scooterette called the Joybike.

"New All-British mo-ped and scooterette the Joybike is now in production."

Manufacturers are H.V.Powell (Cycles) Ltd., of 96-98 Birchfield Road, Birmingham 19. It uses the 49cc Trojan engine with belt primary drive and belt final. The expanding pulley on the primary drive

The first Joybike with the Trojan engine.

gives three speeds to the engine. Wipac lighting and Amal carburettor together with 23 x 2in. Dunlop tyres contribute to this all British machine. In its scooterette form the Joybike is supplied completely enclosed and in the mo-ped form with rear engine cover on near side. 'This is a simple built machine that can't go wrong.' The makers say that all that is required on the subject of servicing is to 'leave it alone'. Apart from cleaning plug and magneto points occasionally, and oiling cables and chains, no other maintenance is necessary. Price: Scooterette £65.0s.0d., mo-ped single gear £55.0s.0d. both include tax.

In 1958 one of the early mopeds cheaper than the Joybike was the clutchless, single gear Raleigh at £48.16.6 – leave that alone too. For a real joy bike another £12 would be necessary to buy the delightful NSU Quickly. In the scooter market with the Joybike Scooterette at £65 another £12 was needed for the Dunkley Popular and £14 for the BSA Dandy – take your choice!

If pedalling a bicycle was really hard work maybe this machine was a 'Joybike' – but it was certainly was not a joy to behold. It was shown in the magazine scooter price lists for just over a year at £65 – perhaps the manufacturers advice of 'leave it alone' was taken too literally. However, more trade news, an updated Joybike was announced for 1961 with a 79cc JAP (J.A.Prestwick) engine and changes to the transmission system – this one never entered the price lists and was never seen again.

REYNOLDS (1958)

Mr Reynolds an ex-Isle of Man racer, with a motorcycle shop in Liverpool, built a prototype machine in the mid 1950s that was called a motor–scooter–cycle by the writer of an article in the Motor Cycling magazine in May 1958. It looked like a large scooter from the front and the rear was totally enclosed, but the engine was in the conventional motorcycle position between the rider's legs.

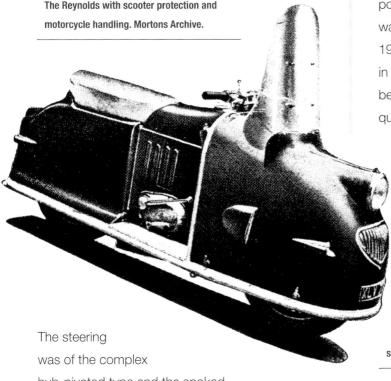

The Reynolds with scooter protection and motorcycle handling. Mortons Archive.

The steering was of the complex hub-pivoted type and the spoked wheels were motorcycle size. The whole machine was constructed around a vast tubular frame and the 250cc twin Villiers engine included a hand starter. All the enclosures were made of sheet steel but glass-fibre panels were planned for the future.

Is it a motorbike?, is it a scooter?, no it is a Maicomobil.

This mix of scooter protection and motorcycle handling had been used before and the most popular machine after the Second World War was made by the German Maico Company in 1951. The Maicomobil used a space frame clad in steel and aluminium with the engine position between the rider's legs, at the start there was a question about was it a motorcycle or a scooter but it soon found its way into the scooter magazines and on to the scooter buyers wish list. Mr Reynolds prototype looked like a fully enclosed heavy motorcycle, and it was unfortunate having produced a good engineering motor–scooter–cycle (but not a very good looking one) that in July 1958 Ariel brought out their new Leader.

Stiff competition for the Reynolds from the streamlined Leader.

This was called sensational at its launch – it was truly good looking – totally enclosed with built in windscreen and pannier bags and also used a new 250cc twin two-stroke engine. It was very quickly advertised in the scooter magazines, 'Why even consider whether you should choose a scooter or a motorcycle when you can have both with the Leader.' It sold quite well over a seven year period but the scooterist missed the step through facility and the proper motorcyclist preferred the bike in its unclad form as the Ariel Arrow. So, Mr Reynolds machine lacked the looks of the Leader and no doubt due to its heavy frame and complex steering would have been more expensive, it therefore never made the production stage.

The DMW company tried this mix in the 1960s with their Deemster with the engine and tank between the rider's legs but the design was not really appreciated by the scooterist or motorcyclist – lucky for DMW it was appreciated by local police patrols. This motor–scooter–cycle may have its day in the future – two wheelers are being developed with electric motor drives obtaining their power from an onboard engine, the wheels may have to be motorcycle size to take an electric motor, the motor and engine may be positioned between the rider's legs and of course it must have full weather protection to appeal to riders and car drivers alike.

This mixed form of propulsion is not new – a young 25 year old Ferdinand Porsche, chief designer for the Austrian family business Lohner, built a car in 1901 called the 'Mixed' with two electric motors in the front wheels and a Daimler petrol engine to power a generator supplying electricity to the two motors. In the 1950s and 60s Lohner made a number of attractive and colourful motor scooters – if only they had developed Porsches 'mixed' they may have been pioneers of the next generation of the 'motor–scooter–cycle'.

STELLA (1958)

In 1958 a small company known as the Stella Motor Scooter Company of Ipswich built a prototype scooter with the front of the machine looking similar to the DMW Bambi. The legshields and footboards were conventional but the engine was exposed with no rear bodywork, therefore it was possible to install the normal air cooled 98cc Villiers motorcycle engine.

Unlike the earlier Bond Gazelle scooter with protective steel strips around the engine the Stella's unit was totally exposed and gave no protection for the rider's clothes. The scooter had large 12" diameter spoked wheels with chrome rims, telescopic front forks and a swinging arm rear suspension.

Late 1950s Stella prototype scooter, IceniCAM Magazine.

98 c.c. ■ ■ ■ ■

STELLA brings you the most exciting Lightweight Machine of the Century

THE STELLA

MINI CYCLE, *a fine example of British Craftsmanship, provides a miniature Motor Cycle of quality, finish and detail normally only found on more expensive machines. Up-to-date styling and practical design are star features of this new idea in two wheeled transportation.*

THE POWER UNIT FOR THIS FINE MACHINE IS A

Villiers

98 c.c. Two Stroke Engine

The handlebars were enhanced with a cowling housing the speedo and horn. It is reported that the Stella was registered in early 1959 – its direct competition in the 98cc scooter range would have been the DMW Bambi and the Sun Geni, no doubt being made by a small company and having the cheaper air cooled engine and no rear bodywork the Stella could have undercut the cost of both of these.

It would then have been competing with the BSA Dandy and the Dunkley S65 – so there may have been room in the market place for such a machine.

Mini Cycle, Ipswich Transport Museum.

A few years later the company did sell a number of small Mini Cycles using 12" wheels and the 98cc engine – these were designed along the lines of the American small motorcycles like the Cushman Eagle that were popular with college boys. A number of these small bikes have survived including one in original condition in the Ipswich Transport museum. It is thought that only one prototype scooter was made and this is not known to survive.

DMW (1959)

At the 1955 London Earls Court Motorcycle Show DMW displayed two new scooters the 98cc Bambi and at the last moment a larger 197cc Dumbo. It took the company until 1957 to move the Bambi to production but the Dumbo was unfortunately never seen again. In 1961 DMW announced their half scooter/half motorcycle called the Deemster, due to its good weather protection and a large storage space under the seat most of the Deemsters spent their existence on Police duties.

The DMW prototype at a VMSC show with the one piece rear bodywork.

However, late in the 1950s DMW designed and made at least one further prototype scooter, compared with the other three scooters this one was a more conventional machine. At this time scooters were being wheeled out by most of the British motorcycle and scooter manufacturers including the joint project between Panther, Sun and Dayton. The prototype made by DMW was from a similar mould as these three – it had the Villiers 175cc fan cooled electric-start engine and the front mudguard and horn housing was similar

to the Panther Princess but the headlamp was positioned on the handlebars. The gear change was the normal heel and toe pedal arrangement and the storage compartments behind the legshields were similar to the Dayton Flamenco, however, the rear bodywork was removed in one piece as opposed to side panels on the other three. Also on the market in 1959 was the glass-fibre Bond P3/P4 and the recently announced BSA and Triumph scooters, and in the wings but late for the party were AMC's James (1960), the new attractive DKR Capella (1960), the big Velocette Viceroy (1961) and the Ambassador scooter (1960).

Perhaps the DMW management looked at the scooters on the road and the machines under development and rightly decided to push the prototype right to the back of the factory. DMW took over Ambassador Motorcycles in 1962 and continued production of some of their motorcycles for a short time but never sold the Ambassador scooter. In 1967 DMW ceased the production of motorcycles but continued to make spares, including Villiers engine spares, and won a government contract to maintain the Villiers engine Invalid Carriages. Finally in the mid 1990s the factory was shut down and the DMW prototype was pulled out from the back, and is now thankfully safe in the hands of a British scooter enthusiast.

NOBLETTA (1960)

During the microcar era of the 1950s the company York Nobel built the German Fundamobil car badged as a Nobel 200 powered by a Sachs

191cc engine. The car had a glass-fibre body and was built by the Bristol Aeroplane Company. Nobel also built a prototype called a Nobletta, this was a three wheeled scooter carrying two people in tandem style, a front screen and canvas roof could be fitted for weather protection.

The Nobletta with front screen and canvas roof. Mortons Archive.

The power source was a 47cc fan cooled Sachs engine positioned over the front wheel with direct drive, for protection and decoration a wire grill was built over the engine. In November 1960 the company said a commercial version was also planned and prices would be announced soon. Although the Nobel 200 microcar was very attractive in its two tone paintwork with a sunshine roof many manufacturing problems arose and very few were sold. The little three wheeler Nobletta was never seen again.

The Nobel 200 with a Sachs 191cc engine.

ROYAL ENFIELD FANTABULOUS (1961)

The Royal Enfield bicycle manufacturer started building motorcycles in the early 1900s, following World War Two they won an order from the Indian Government for their 350cc motorcycle for armed forces and police duties. In 1955 Madras Motors of India were assembling the Royal Enfield motorcycle under licence and by 1957 were manufacturing the machine.

The Royal Enfield Fantabulus scooter
looking a bit like the Panther Princess.

In the late 1950s Royal Enfield and Enfield India were working with the Villiers engine company to produce a scooter. This machine looked a little like the Panther Princess and was to be manufactured and sold in India, by 1961 an agreement had been made between Enfield India and Villiers for the scooters 175cc Villiers engine to be manufactured in India. In the Villiers magazine of Autumn 1961 a picture was shown of the scooter stating 'the Villiers-powered scooter being made by Enfield India is based on the P & M Panther Princess, one of the best-looking of the British Scooters.'

The scooter was named the Fantabulous in India and differed from the British Princess by having the headlamp on the handlebars and a one piece rear body with no side panels, (maintenance was achieved by raising the seat or completely removing the rear bodywork), but it did have the same Villiers 175cc engine with an electric-start

and two pedal gear change as the Princess. The machine was produced through the 1960s but was never sold in Great Britain. However, it has been reported that the scooter was shown on the Royal Enfield stand at the 1968 London Earls Court Show. The manufacture of all British scooters had ceased in the mid 1960s, and in 1967 Royal Enfield were in trouble and had been taken over by Norton-Villiers so perhaps showing the scooter in 1968 was an attempt to help the companies financial situation. The Fantabulous scooter is now a rare machine even in India.

The manufacture of British Royal Enfield motorcycles finally ended in 1971, however Royal Enfield India still produce the 500cc machine in a much updated form and export it to the UK, Europe, USA and Australia.

POST 1970 SCOOTERS

Many of the British scooters were discontinued during the early 1960s with a few, including the BSA/Triumph and DKR Capella, lasting until the mid 1960s. In Germany the Heinkel, Maicoletta and Zundapp Bella all finished in the mid 1960s with just the Zundapp 50cc scooter being produced until the mid 1980s. Production of the Italian Innocenti Lambretta ceased in 1971 with the Lambretta continuing to be made in Spain and India. The only manufacturer that started in 1946 and still produces scooters today is Piaggio of Italy making of course the Vespa.

The very modern 1986 Honda Spacy 250 scooter recently purchased by the author.

The 1970s through to the 1990s was a lean time for scooters with the sports moped of the 70s satisfying the youth market at that time and the Japanese step-through satisfying the commuters, throughout this period Vespas were still being produced in the 125 to 200cc range. However, in the early 1980s Honda announced their Spacy 125 with futuristic styling and twist and go transmission, also in 1983 Honda introduced the three wheeled Stream scooter based on the tilting arrangement of the earlier British Ariel 3 – the Stream was still only 50cc but a far better engineered machine. By the mid 1980s the larger Spacy 250 was on sale and other Japanese

and European manufacturers were planning to bring further scooters to the market. The Honda Spacy 250 had a 250cc four-stroke liquid cooled engine with automatic clutch and gears, automatic fuel tap and choke, self-cancelling indicators and as the name suggests futuristic styling with a top speed of 70 mph. It also had tubeless tyres with a front hydraulic brake and digital speedo and clock. For security there was a handbrake and locks for the steering, seat and for two helmets. With the ignition off by pressing the horn button a light located the ignition key switch for the rider! It just needed two extras – a screen and top box – to make it a real modern 'car on two wheels'. Honda were leading the way in the 1980s for the new breed of twist and go scooters that fill the roads today.

A 2005 large wheel Aprilia Scarabeo with 250cc engine and linked brakes.

As the 1990s progressed Yamaha introduced their Majesty 250 with feet forward style and a four-stroke engine capable of 75 mph. Suzuki followed with their Burgman initially with a 250cc engine and then a 400cc making it a 100mph scooter.

Piaggio's engineering marvel, the MP3 three wheel tilting scooter.

The Italian manufacturers such as Aprilia with their large wheel Scarabeo range and Gilera with a sporty 180cc Runner were also moving fast to satisfy a new scooter market. Traffic congestion, pollution, ease of travel and style were creating this new market.

A 1951 Vespa 125cc two-stroke with cable drum brakes.

By the end of the 1990s scooters had real style and their technical specifications included modern four-stroke water cooled engines, luxury suspension/ seating and storage space for helmets. Some of the bright ideas from earlier scooters were turned into engineering realities – a scooter with a roof, used by 'Spike' Rhiando to tackle the Sahara Desert in 1953, was built by BMW with a safety cage and a seat belt with the plan of freeing riders of a safety helmet. Benelli also produced a roofed scooter that cleverly

folded into the rear top box when not required. Ariel's tilting three wheeler was totally changed into an engineering marvel by Piaggio with its MP3 having two wheels at the front, these scooters can now be seen with blues and twos being used by the police in London. Electric scooters appeared on the market following the path started by Mr Ridley in 1948 and Mr Winn with his City Bike in 1965.

So, since 1946 scooters have travelled from 98/125cc air cooled two-stroke engines into 50/850cc quiet and efficient four-stroke water cooled units, brakes from cable and drum to hydraulic and disc – sometimes with two discs on the front wheel and sometimes linked brakes – metal bodies have moved through glass-fibre to plastic (except the Vespa) and storage capacity has grown from a sandwich box to as large as the original BMC Mini boot, and most of course have electric starters.

A 2009 Vespa 125cc four-stroke with a front hydraulic disc brake.

No doubt the future will bring more electric driven machines – some with small generators to recharge the batteries on the move to increase the range – and maybe the new three wheeled scooters will include a roof and move in the direction of a much improved cabin scooter of the 1950/60s. Maybe the F.I.M. (Federation Internationale Motocycliste) will have to review its 'definition of a scooter'.

THE CLASSIC SCOOTER SCENE TODAY

The collecting, riding and restoration of scooters from the 1950/60s period is encouraged and supported today by many clubs. The Vintage Motor Scooter Club (VMSC) was set up in 1985 'to cater for the needs of the scooter enthusiast who is interested in the preservation and restoration of these machines' this has successfully been accomplished by producing a bi-monthly magazine including advice, specialist information, technical data and small advertisements for sales and wants.

The VMSC stand was awarded 1st prize at the 2010 Stafford Motorcycle Show.

The club also arranges a full programme of rallies and attendances at various shows including the top Motorcycle Shows and Steam Rallies. For years the VMSC has provided show stands at the large Bristol and Stafford Motorcycle Shows, and scooters on club rallies range from 125cc Vespas to the large 250cc Maicoletta and Viceroy machines – modern twist and go scooters are also welcome.

Some of the smaller capacity scooters with engine sizes under 100cc join the rallies organised by the NACC. The National Autocycle and Cyclemotor Club was formed in 1981 as the East Anglian Cyclemotor Club. Since its inception the club has grown and now has members all over the British Isles and other parts of the World. Again the NACC has an excellent magazine called 'Buzzing' and a very full programme of events and rallies where scooters such as the BSA Dandy or a rare DMW Bambi can be seen on a run. The NACC also has an extremely comprehensive library dealing with most two-wheelers under 100cc and in particular Cyclemotors, Autocycles and Mopeds.

VMSC Derbyshire rally at the National Tram Museum 2011.

The Velocette Viceroy scooter is one of the machines welcomed by the Velocette LE Club, the Bond scooters take part in events held by the Bond Owner's Club, and all two-stroke scooters are welcomed by the British Two Stroke Club.

This club is for enthusiasts of all types of two wheelers that are powered by two-stroke engines of any capacity, the BTSC was founded in 1929 and covers any make/model that was manufactured in Britain or imported into Britain.

Excelsior Heinkel joins Diana Treffen in Germany 2011.

In addition to the clubs that cater for any make of scooter there are also a number of one-make clubs. Clubs exist for the Italian Lambretta, Vespa and Moto Rumi and others for the German Maico and Zundapp Bella scooters.

Even the dog (toy) joins in the rally fun, Amberley Scooter day 2007.

Again these clubs have magazines, specialists and a programme of events, the clubs also have strong links with the country of manufacture with German owners attending rallies in Britain and club members joining the rallies (treffens) in Germany.

Many local scooter clubs also exist in Britain for classic and modern scooters – some of these clubs can trace their history back to the 1950s. Most clubs are involved in charity work and many scooters join with motorcycles on runs at Easter and Christmas taking eggs and toys to Children's Hospitals – the days of conflict between the Mods and Rockers of the mid 1960s are long gone. It is also not unusual to see Heinkel bubble cars and other microcars taking part in scooter rallies.

Restorations like this rare Cezeta scooter from the former Czechoslovakia are now possible with club and Internet support.

Only a short time ago in the 1980s most classic scooter enthusiasts would have difficulties finding information and spares to restore a scooter from the 1950/60s, however, with the current active club scene and Internet assistance from around the World even the restoration of a rare Czech scooter is certainly feasible today.

Durkopp Diana – powerful, good road holding and elegant.

USEFUL WEBSITES

Bond Owners Club	www.bondownersclub.co.uk
British Two Stroke Club	www.britishtwostrokeclub.org.uk
Coventry Transport Museum	www.transport-museum.com
IceniCAM Magazine	www.icenicam.ukfsn.org
Ipswich Transport Museum	www.ipswichtransportmuseum.co.uk
Lambretta Club of GB	www.ilambretta.com
London Motorcycle Museum	www.london-motorcycle-museum.org
Maico Scooter Club	www.maico.org.uk
Moto Rumi Scooter Club	www.motorumiclub.co.uk
National Autocycle & Cyclemotor Club	www.thebuzzingclub.co.uk
Register of Unusual Microcars	www.rumcars.org
The British Motorcycle Charitable Trust	www.bmct.org
The Invalid Carriage Register	www.invalidcarriageregister.wordpress.com
The Trojan Museum Trust	www.trojanmuseumtrust.org
The Vintage Motor Cycle Club	www.vmcc.net
Vespa Club of GB	www.vespaclubofbritain.co.uk
Velocette LE Club	www.leveloclub.org.uk
Vintage Motor Scooter Club	www.vmsc.co.uk
Zundapp Bella Scooter Club	www.zundappbella.co.uk

East German, Berlin/Troll

125cc Coco Taxi

Russian Tula 3 wheeler

Some classic scooters are still used today and miss out on the rally scene, Cuba 2011.

178

CONCLUSION
THE BRITISH MOTOR SCOOTER

The first British motor scooter produced after the Second World War was the Swallow Gadabout made by a sidecar company with a pre-war Villiers engine. One of the last British scooters made was the DKR Capella, produced by a company set-up in 1957 – specifically to make motor scooters – also with a Villiers engine. Some of the earliest scooters produced in Britain were made by cycle manufacturers including Dayton and Mercury, new companies such as DKR, Bond and Phoenix, the motor accessory company Britax and even a coach-built perambulator maker Dunkley. None were made by the experienced British motorcycle manufacturers.

engines with cooling fans and electric start enabled some of the design constraints to be lifted for British scooter manufacturers.

Unlike the British motorcycle industry the Europeans moved into scooter production much earlier – in Italy MV Augusta made a scooter in 1949, Moto Guzzi in 1950 and Ducati and Parilla in 1952. In Germany NSU were making the Italian Lambretta under licence from 1950, Maico sold their first scooter in 1951 and Zundapp in 1953. The French motorcycle company Terrot made a scooter in 1951 and Peugeot in 1953, and Austria's Puch Motorcycle company began scooter manufacturing in 1952.

Shame the BSA Beeza did not reach production.

Shame Britax did not use this attractive Casalini body with the superb Ducati Cucciolo engine for their Scooterette.

Most of these early scooters used proprietary Villiers engines made for the motorcycle industry – so early scooters had a number of design constraints including chain drive to the rear wheel, no cooling fan and no electric start. Swallow had to fit a car type fan to adequately cool the engine of their Gadabout and Dayton had to build a cooling tunnel to solve their cooling problems with the 225cc Villiers engine. However, soon the Government requirements for the Invalid Carriage Industry to fit

In Britain one of the first real scooters made by the British motorcycle industry in 1957 – the Bambi – was made by the small motorcycle manufacturer DMW with a Villiers engine. It was not until 1958 the large BSA group made the BSA Sunbeam/ Triumph Tigress scooters using their own engines. Following this an avalanche of British motorcycle manufacturers at last came up with a scooter.

These included the Sun Wasp, Panther Princess, Excelsior Monarch, Velocette Viceroy, Ambassador and even the AMC group (including Matchless/AJS motorcycles) made the James scooter. Unfortunately, it was at least five years too late – some of these machines were on the market for only two or three years and a small number limped on to the mid 1960s. What a shame.

What a shame the BSA Dinghy prototype with a semi-automatic transmission did not make it to production in the 1940s. What a shame the attractive BSA Beeza shown in 1955 did not reach production. What a shame the Britax Scooterette with the superb Ducati Cucciolo engine did not use the attractive Italian Casalini body (as used by Dunkley in later years) instead of their own ugly body. What a shame the attractive DKR Capella did not replace the odd looking Dove a few years earlier and what a shame Dayton got involved with a Holding Company that stopped the development of their attractive 250cc Continental Twin.

a top speed near running pace the rider had to be sixteen, pass a driving test and the modified bicycle had to be registered , taxed and insured. So most of the early cyclemotors were made by specialist companies such as EMI's Cyclemaster and Trojan's Mini-Motor. European countries were more relaxed with the driving age and registration of the machines, also both cyclemotors and mopeds were able to use the cycle lanes as they do today.

When the sale of mopeds replaced the cyclemotor market it was the bicycle companies such as Philips, Hercules and Raleigh that spearheaded the sales, then the same thing happened with the scooter with the motorcycle industry dragging its feet. The one British motorcycle company that did act quickly was Douglas who made the Italian Piaggio Vespa under licence – unfortunately because of their manufacturing facilities they failed to meet Piaggio targets which allowed Lambretta imports by the efficient Lambretta Concessionaires Ltd to outsell the Vespa.

Shame the very attractive DKR Capella did not replace the odd looking Dove sooner.

Shame Dayton got involved with a Holding Company that stopped their future expansion plans.

The Government did little to help the British Motorcycle Industry get the first time buyer onto British machines. Although before the war a cheaper road tax was introduced for machines under 100cc (which gave birth to the British Autocycle) there was no relaxation following the war to encourage the Industry to make cyclemotors or mopeds. Even to ride a cyclemotor with an engine size of 18cc and

In the early 1950s when European motorcycle companies were producing scooters the British motorcycle industry had full order books for larger bikes, and unfortunately elderly machine tools and factories plus elderly management that appeared to had no five year plan and enjoyed making what they liked to make. It has been reported that even as late as 1970 only 10% of British bosses had any formal qualifications in Management. The British motorcycle industry also had a past, this was something a small company operating out of a shed in Japan did not have. In 1961 Soichiro Honda is quoted as saying 'I started with 50 employees. That was in 1948. Now we have 5,500 employees. Honda has no past. We only have a future. We would not be able to do business if we were provided only with the past. The customers demanded quality – not history.' In 1958 both Honda and the whole of the British motorcycle industry produced a similar number of units – 200,000, however, ten years later the British industry made approximately 80,000 and Honda 1.5 million. In the late 1950s Honda produced a

little two-wheeler, a cross between a moped and a scooter called the Super Cub, by 2010 they had made 70 million.

Due to the 'history' of the British Motorcycle Industry with its world beating bikes of a previous golden age the industry failed to meet the challenge of the post war cyclemotor, moped and unfortunately the British scooter.

ACKNOWLEDGEMENTS

My scooter collecting and the restoration works carried out since 1999 would not have been possible without the help of other collectors and friends. When there was no further room in my garage for scooters a large log cabin was built in 2001 in the rear garden and the picture – taken when the cabin was opened – shows the friends that assisted my scooter collecting. This includes from the left:- Martin Plummer, James Diehl, Mike Webster, Graham Mitchell, Mike Dan, (Robin Spalding) and Eddie Marley. Eddie sold me my Dayton Albatross scooter in 1960, and various other machines since, he owned Greyhound Motorcycles in Croydon, Surrey from the 1950s until the shop unfortunately became a victim of the Croydon riots in August 2011. The scooters from the left are a German Zundapp Bella, a German Heinkel Tourist A2 and a British Dayton Albatross.

Scooter log cabin December 2010

Producing a book featuring colourful scooters obviously demanded good quality photographs taken by a professional. This was a challenge – a large garage and the log cabin were packed full of scooters with many on platforms above ground level. Each machine would have to be removed and placed in a light-tent for the photographs to be taken. The picture shows the heavy lifting gang with Stewart the photographer sitting, my wife Eileen on the Triumph Tigress with John and Peter standing at the back, the work took a full weekend with Eileen providing refreshments over the two days. At a later date the light-tent was taken to the London Motorcycle Museum at Greenford to photograph the six scooters from the collection currently in Bill Crosby's museum. The picture shows Bill and his wife Philippa with the BSA Sunbeam 250.

Bill and Philippa Crosby at the London Motorcycle Museum with the BSA Sunbeam.

The light-tent in the garage ready for pictures of the Tigress 250.

The following organisations and people have also helped with information/photographs:

- **The Vintage Motor Scooter Club**, especially the long serving Chairman Ian Harrop his wife Marge and the club historian Mike Webster.

- **The Vintage Motor Cycle Club** for pictures and information on the BSA Dinghy and DMW Bambi.

- **Mortons Archive** for images from Motor Cycling and The Motor Cycle magazines.

- **Coventry Transport Museum** for pictures of the Ridley scooter and Kieft racing car.

- **Ipswich Transport Museum** for information and pictures of the Stella Mini Cycle.

- **Stewart Darkes** for photographing the scooter collection, www.inphotopia.com

- **Stewart Simpson** (Scooter Stu) for photographs and brochures from his large collection of scooter memorabilia. www.punksinparkas.com

- The late **Jack Tattersall** for selling me the rare Britax scooterette from his fine transport collection, and using pictures of the American Doodle Bug scooter and the Honda Goldwing trike.

- **Lucy Davidson** for drawing the cartoon of the Dunkley Pramotor (lucy@peasandneedles.co.uk)

- Many of the scooter pictures shown have been collected over a lifetime and permission has been sought for use in the book. Therefore I apologise if I have not been able to establish the true source of any of the pictures.

Again none of the book preparation would have been possible without the support and encouragement given by my wife Eileen. Over the last four years Eileen has spent hours at the keyboard working on the text and page layout, and having the patience to teach me to do some of it myself. Now she is able to pick out a British scooter at 20 yards and put a name to it – however, she did surprise me recently when she mentioned a Douglas Lambretta instead of the more popular Douglas Vespa!

Some of the British scooter collection.

INDEX

Mercury Pippin
page 53

Excelsior Monarch MKII page103

Vintage Motor Scooter Club stand at the Stafford Show 2008